Lecture Notes in Computer Science 15425

Founding Editors

Gerhard Goos
Juris Hartmanis

The series Lecture Notes in Computer Science (LNCS), including its subseries Lecture Notes in Artificial Intelligence (LNAI) and Lecture Notes in Bioinformatics (LNBI), has established itself as a medium for the publication of new developments in computer science and information technology research, teaching, and education.

LNCS enjoys close cooperation with the computer science R & D community, the series counts many renowned academics among its volume editors and paper authors, and collaborates with prestigious societies. Its mission is to serve this international community by providing an invaluable service, mainly focused on the publication of conference and workshop proceedings and postproceedings. LNCS commenced publication in 1973.

Jun Feng · Songlin He · Liang-Jie Zhang
Editors

Blockchain –
ICBC 2024

7th International Conference
Held as Part of the Services Conference Federation, SCF 2024
Bangkok, Thailand, November 16–19, 2024
Proceedings

 Springer

Editors
Jun Feng ⓘ
Huazhong University of Science
and Technology
Wuhan, China

Songlin He ⓘ
Southwest Jiaotong University
Chengdu, China

Liang-Jie Zhang ⓘ
Shenzhen University
Shenzhen, China

ISSN 0302-9743 ISSN 1611-3349 (electronic)
Lecture Notes in Computer Science
ISBN 978-3-031-77094-4 ISBN 978-3-031-77095-1 (eBook)
https://doi.org/10.1007/978-3-031-77095-1

Preface

The International Conference on Blockchain (ICBC) aims to provide an international forum for both researchers and industry practitioners to exchange the latest fundamental advances in the state-of-the-art technologies and best practices of blockchain, as well as emerging standards and research topics which will define the future of blockchain.

ICBC 2024 was a member of the Services Conference Federation (SCF). SCF 2024 had the following 10 collocated service-oriented sister conferences: 2024 International Conference on Web Services (ICWS 2024), 2024 International Conference on Cloud Computing (CLOUD 2024), 2024 International Conference on Services Computing (SCC 2024), 2024 International Conference on Big Data (BigData 2024), 2024 International Conference on AI & Multimodal Services (AIMS 2024), 2024 International Conference on Metaverse (METAVERSE 2024), 2024 International Conference on Internet of Things (ICIOT 2024), 2024 International Conference on Cognitive Computing (ICCC 2024), 2024 International Conference on Edge Computing (EDGE 2024), and 2024 International Conference on Blockchain (ICBC 2024). As the founding member of SCF, the first International Conference on Web Services (ICWS) was held in June 2003 in Las Vegas, USA. Meanwhile, the First International Conference on Web Services - Europe 2003 (ICWS-Europe 2003) was held in Germany in October 2003. ICWS-Europe 2003 was an extended event of the 2003 International Conference on Web Services (ICWS 2003) in Europe. In 2004, ICWS-Europe was changed to the European Conference on Web Services (ECOWS), which was held at Erfurt, Germany.

This volume presents the accepted papers of the 2024 International Conference on Blockchain (ICBC 2024), held in Bangkok, Thailand during November 16–19, 2024. For this conference, each paper was single-blind reviewed by three independent members of the International Program Committee. After carefully evaluating their originality and quality, we accepted 9 papers.

We are pleased to thank the authors whose submissions and participation made this conference possible. We also want to express our thanks to the Organizing Committee and Program Committee members, for their dedication in helping to organize the conference and reviewing the 20 submissions. We owe special thanks to the keynote speakers for their impressive speeches.

Finally, we would like to thank operations team members Jing Zeng, Sheng He, Yishuang Ning, and Zhuolin Mei for their excellent work in organizing this conference. We look forward to your future great contributions as a volunteer, author, and conference participant in the fast-growing worldwide services innovations community.

September 2024

Jun Feng
Songlin He
Liang-Jie Zhang

Organization

General Chair

Kai Lei — Peking University, China

Program Chairs

Jun Feng — Huazhong University of Science and Technology, China

Songlin He — Southwest Jiaotong University, China

Services Conference Federation (SCF 2024)

General Chairs

Ali Arsanjani — Google, USA

Wu Chou — Essenlix Corporation, USA

Coordinating Program Chair

Liang-Jie Zhang — Shenzhen University, China

CFO and International Affairs Chair

Min Luo — Georgia Tech, USA

Operation Committee

Jing Zeng — China Gridcom Co., Ltd., China

Yishuang Ning — Tsinghua University, China

Sheng He — Kingdee International Software Group Co., Ltd., China

Zhuolin Mei — Jiujiang University, China

Steering Committee

Calton Pu (Co-chair)   Georgia Tech, USA
Liang-Jie Zhang (Co-chair)   Shenzhen University, China

ICBC 2024 Program Committee

Babu Pillai   Southern Cross University, Australia
Xinxin Fan   IoTeX, USA
Adel Elmessiry   WebDBTech, USA
Rudrapatna K. Shyamasundar   Indian Institute of Technology Bombay, India
Lei Xu   Kent State University, USA
Roberto Di Pietro   King Abdullah University of Science and
                               Technology, Saudi Arabia
Jo-Ann Magsumbol   Polytechnic University of the Philippines,
                               Philippines
Mike McBride   Futurewei Technologies, USA
Rui Zhang   Institute of Information Engineering, Chinese
                               Academy of Sciences, China
Shiping Chen   Commonwealth Scientific and Industrial Research
                               Organisation, Australia
Kazumasa Omote   University of Tsukuba, Japan
Dirk Trossen   Huawei Technologies Düsseldorf GmbH,
                               Germany
Andreas Veneris   University of Toronto, Canada
Gang Wang   University of Connecticut, USA

Conference Sponsor – Services Society

The Services Society (S2) is a non-profit professional organization that has been created to promote worldwide research and technical collaboration in services innovations among academia and industrial professionals. Its members are volunteers from industry and academia with common interests. S2 is registered in the USA as a "501(c) organization", which means that it is an American tax-exempt nonprofit organization. S2 collaborates with other professional organizations to sponsor or co-sponsor conferences and to promote an effective services curriculum in colleges and universities. S2 initiates and promotes a "Services University" program worldwide to bridge the gap between industrial needs and university instruction.

The Services Sector accounted for 79.5% of the GDP of the USA in 2016. The Services Society has formed 5 Special Interest Groups (SIGs) to support technology- and domain-specific professional activities.

- Special Interest Group on Services Computing (SIG-SC)
- Special Interest Group on Big Data (SIG-BD)
- Special Interest Group on Cloud Computing (SIG-CLOUD)
- Special Interest Group on Artificial Intelligence (SIG-AI)
- Special Interest Group on Metaverse (SIG-Metaverse)

About the Services Conference Federation (SCF)

As the founding member of the Services Conference Federation (SCF), the first **International Conference on Web Services (ICWS)** was held in June 2003 in Las Vegas, USA. Meanwhile, the First International Conference on Web Services - Europe 2003 (ICWS-Europe 2003) was held in Germany in October 2003. ICWS-Europe 2003 was an extended event of the 2003 International Conference on Web Services (ICWS 2003) in Europe. In 2004, ICWS-Europe was changed to the European Conference on Web Services (ECOWS), which was held at Erfurt, Germany. Sponsored by the Services Society and Springer, SCF 2018 and SCF 2019 were held successfully in Seattle and San Diego, USA. SCF 2020 and SCF 2021 were held successfully online and in Shenzhen, China. SCF 2022 and 2023 were held successfully in Hawaii, USA. To celebrate its 22nd birthday, SCF 2024 was held on November 16–19, 2024, Bangkok, Thailand.

In the past 21 years, the ICWS community has expanded from Web engineering innovations to scientific research for the whole services industry. Service delivery platforms have been expanded to mobile platforms, Internet of Things, cloud computing, and edge computing. The services ecosystem has gradually been enabled, value added, and intelligence embedded through enabling technologies such as big data, artificial intelligence, and cognitive computing. In the coming years, all the transactions with multiple parties involved will be transformed to blockchain.

Based on the technology trends and best practices in the field, the Services Conference Federation (SCF) will continue serving as the conference umbrella's code name for all services-related conferences. SCF 2024 defined the future of New ABCDE (AI, Blockchain, Cloud, BigData & IOT) and entered the 5G for Services Era. The theme of ICWS 2024 was Web-based Services for Metaverse Era. We are very proud to announce that SCF 2024's 10 co-located theme topic conferences all-centered around "services", with each focusing on exploring different themes (web-based services, cloud-based services, Big Data-based services, services innovation lifecycle, AI-driven ubiquitous services, blockchain driven trust service-ecosystems, industry-specific services and applications, and emerging service-oriented technologies).

- Bigger Platform: The 10 collocated conferences (SCF 2024) were sponsored by the Services Society, which is the world-leading not-for-profit organization (501 c(3)) dedicated for the service of more than 30,000 worldwide Services Computing researchers and practitioners. A bigger platform means bigger opportunities for all volunteers, authors, and participants. Meanwhile, Springer provided sponsorship to best paper awards and other professional activities. All the 10 conference proceedings of SCF 2024 were published by Springer and indexed in ISI Conference Proceedings Citation Index (included in Web of Science), Engineering Index EI (Compendex and Inspec databases), DBLP, Google Scholar, IO-Port, MathSciNet, Scopus, and ZBlMath.
- Brighter Future: While celebrating the 2024 version of ICWS, SCF 2024 highlighted the International Conference on AI and Multimodal Services (AIMS 2024) to build

the fundamental infrastructure for enabling AIGC services ecosystems. It will also
lead our community members to create their own brighter future.

– Better Model: SCF 2024 continued to leverage the invented Conference Blockchain
  Model (CBM) to innovate the organizing practices for all the 10 theme conferences.
  Senior researchers in the field are welcome to submit proposals to serve as CBM
  Ambassador for an individual conference to start better interactions during your
  leadership role in for organizing future SCF conferences.

Contents

Research Track

Enabling a Smooth Migration Towards Post-Quantum Security
for Ethereum 3
    Xinxin Fan, Teik Guan Tan, Nicholas Ho, and Shi Hong Choy

Accelerating Blockchain Application Development: Integrating
Blockchain as a Service Within Low-Code Platforms 16
    Sheng He, Qinglin Huang, Shaoshuai Jiao, Zepeng Lin, Jinxuan Lin,
    Jun Ren, Dengbin Xiong, and Liang-Jie Zhang

Legacy Compatible and Sybil Resistant Decentralized Identity
Management for IoTs 33
    Songlin He, Xukang Lyu, and Dongliang Chu

Enhancing Robustness of Smart Contracts Through Declarations 50
    R. K. Shyamasundar, Snehal Borse, and Mohammad Ummair

Novel Perpetual Futures Market Model Based on a Family of Asymptotic
Power Curves 69
    Thuat Do, Tuan-Anh Pham, and Tuan Tran

Improving Raft Consensus Algorithm with Relay and Lease Mechanism 84
    Yufang Sun, Bing Guo, Daiwei Jia, and Songlin He

Towards Pediatric Healthcare: A Blockchain-Based Framework
for Transparent and Secure Medical Data Management 95
    H. V. Khanh, T. D. Khoa, T. K. N. Ngan, V. C. P. Loc, N. H. Bang,
    N. T. Anh, N. N. Hung, and M. N. Triet

SoK on Blockchain Evolution and Taxonomy 109
    Thuat Do and Dinh-Ngoc Bui

Application and Industry Track

Cadastral: Blockchain-Based Land Registration System 123
    Sagar Suresh, Kevin Van, Chandan Yadav, Merlin Jacob,
    and Varsha Wangikar

Author Index 137

Research Track

Enabling a Smooth Migration Towards Post-Quantum Security for Ethereum

Xinxin Fan[1]([✉])(ⓘ), Teik Guan Tan[2](ⓘ), Nicholas Ho[2], and Shi Hong Choy[2]

[1] IoTeX, Menlo Park, CA 94025, USA
xinxin@iotex.io
[2] pQCee Pte Ltd., Singapore 038987, Singapore
{**teikguan,nicholasho,shihong**}**@pqcee.com**

Abstract. Digital signatures based on Elliptic Curve Digital Signing Algorithm (ECDSA) are widely used in Ethereum to secure transactions and Proof-of-Stake (PoS) consensus protocols. However, those digital signatures are vulnerable to quantum computing and therefore endanger the security of Ethereum and its millions of users' crypto assets. Based on the previous work in [16,17], we present two proposals for a smooth migration of Ethereum towards post-quantum security in this paper. While the first proposal introduces a new Ethereum transaction type to encapsulate a quantum-safe zero-knowledge proof, the second one further improves system scalability via proof aggregation and zero-knowledge rollups. Our proposals only introduce minimal changes to the software running on Ethereum validators and clients, thereby achieving great backward compatibility. We report our initial evaluation results of the two proposals on Microsoft's Azure cloud platform and highlight the key observations, in the area of improving proof generation timing and proof sizes, for deploying our solutions in practice.

Keywords: Ethereum · ECDSA · Post-Quantum Security · Migration

1 Introduction

With the possibility of large-scale quantum computing on the horizon, blockchain systems (e.g., Ethereum) that are currently secured by elliptic curve cryptography could become vulnerable to a quantum attacker. As shown in Fig. 1, ECDSA has been extensively used in Ethereum for users signing transactions, validators verifying transactions in a PoS consensus process, among other use cases. Once a user has made a transaction with his/her Ethereum wallet, a quantum attacker is able to recover the user's private key using Shor's algorithm [15] and steal all the assets from the user's wallet. As a result, migrating Ethereum towards post-quantum security is a critical step for protecting users' crypto assets in the near future.

The National Institute of Science and Technology (NIST) has been working on the Post-Quantum Cryptography project [12] during the past seven years

J. Feng et al. (Eds.): ICBC 2024, LNCS 15425, pp. 3–15, 2025.
https://doi.org/10.1007/978-3-031-77095-1_1

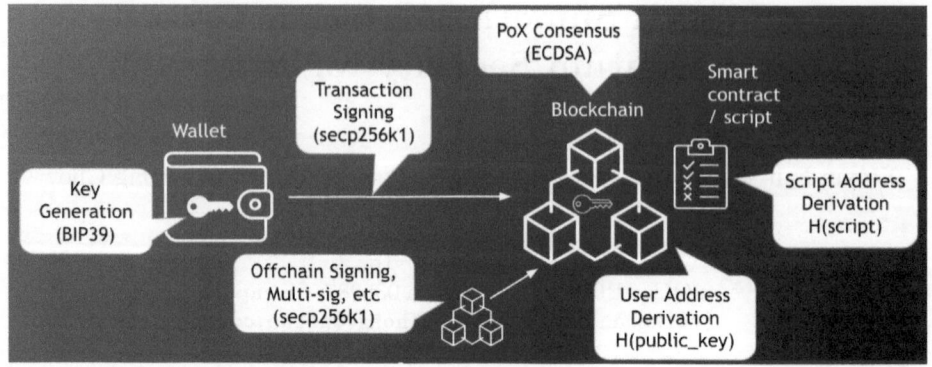

Fig. 1. The Usage of ECDSA in Ethereum

for soliciting, evaluating, and standardizing quantum-resistant public-key cryptographic algorithms. In the Ethereum research community, there was a proposal [11] regarding adoption of NIST standardized quantum-safe signature
algorithm Falcon in Ethereum. Recent post [2] by Vitalik Buterin has further
highlighted importance of migrating Ethereum towards post-quantum security.
In [16], Tan and Zhou proposed a novel generic construction of quantum-safe
signature algorithms by augmenting a classical digital signature with a quantum-
resistant zero-knowledge proof of knowledge of the pre-image of the private signing key using ZKBoo [7]. For verifying such a quantum-safe signature, a verifier
needs to verify validity of both the classical signature and corresponding zero-
knowledge proof. In [17], Tan and Zhou further analyzed the impact for migrating
blockchain away from ECDSA for post-quantum security.

In this paper, we present two proposals to enable a smooth migration
towards post-quantum security for Ethereum. Our proposals are built upon the
quantum-safe signature algorithm proposed in [16]. The first proposal covers
how Ethereum at Layer-1 can be updated to be post-quantum secure by natively
verifying every additional quantum-resistant zero-knowledge proof submitted by
the users. The second proposal further improves on scalability of the first one
by leveraging zk-Rollups coupled with a tree-based recursive proof aggregation
process. In particular, our proposals align well with the current implementations
of Ethereum validators and clients and therefore achieve great backward compatibility. The initial performance evaluation results demonstrates a path for
deploying our solution in practice.

The rest of the paper is organized as follows: In Sect. 2, we present some
preliminaries, followed by the detailed description and implementation considerations of our two migration proposals in Sect. 3. Section 4 evaluates the performance of our migration proposals and highlights the key observations with
respect to the real-world deployment. Finally, we conclude the paper in Sect. 5.

2   Preliminaries

In this section, we cover the preliminaries on quantum-safe digital signature algorithms and zero-knowledge proofs, Ethereum transactions, and zk-rollups.

2.1   Quantum-Safe Digital Signature Algorithms

In [16], Tan and Zhou described a novel approach for layering in quantum-resistance into classical digital signature algorithms like ECDSA by applying quantum-safe zero-knowledge proofs on the pre-image of the private signing key. The proposed generic quantum-resistant digital signature scheme consists of the following three algorithms:

- **KeyGen**$_q(1^n)$ → $\{\rho, K_p\}$ takes in a security parameter 1^n which defines the cryptographic key strength of n, and outputs a secret pre-image ρ and a public key K_p. K_p is the associated public key to the private key $H(\rho)$ where $H(\cdot)$ is a collapsing hash function [19][1]
- **Sign**$_q(M, \rho)$ → $\{\sigma, \phi\}$ takes in a message M and the secret pre-image ρ, and outputs a signature σ computed using the classical signature algorithm **Sign**$(M, H(\rho))$ as well as a quantum-resistant zero-knowledge proof ϕ that i) $H(\rho)$ is computed from ρ and ii) σ is computed from $H(\rho)$.
- **Verify**$_q(M, K_p, \sigma, \phi)$ → $\{result\}$ takes in a message M, the public key K_p and signature σ, and outputs accept if and only if the classical signature verification algorithm **Verify**(M, K_p) returns accept and ϕ is a valid zero-knowledge proof that σ is computed from ρ.

The above construction is able to achieve quantum resistance while maintaining backward compatibility with existing classical digital signature implementations.

2.2   Ethereum Transactions

An Ethereum transaction refers to an action initiated by an externally-owned account (EOA). As of Ethereum's London upgrade, there are three transaction types: 0x0 (EIP-2718 [21]), 0x1 (EIP-2930 [5]), and 0x2 (EIP-1559 [3]). Transactions with type 0x0 are legacy transactions that contain the following parameters:

- **nonce**: A sequentially incrementing counter which indicates the transaction number from the account;
- **gasPrice**: The number of Wei to be paid per unit of gas for conducting a transaction or executing a contract;
- **gasLimit**: The maximum amount of gas units that can be consumed by the transaction;
- **to**: The 160-bit receiving address;
- **value**: The number of Wei to transfer from sender to recipient;

---

[1] Collapsing hash functions are defined to be collision-resistant in the face of quantum attacks.

– **data**: The optional field to include arbitrary data;
– **v, r, s**: The signature of the transaction used for determining the identifier of the sender.

Transactions with type 0x1 were introduced in EIP-2930 and contain, along with the legacy parameters, an **accessList** parameter. Each access list is a tuple of an account address and a list of storage keys that the transaction plans to access. Finally, transactions with type 0x2 were introduced in EIP-1559 for addressing the network congestion and overpricing of transaction fees caused by the historical fee market. To this end, EIP-1559 replaces **gasPrice** in legacy transactions with an in-protocol, dynamically changing base fee per gas at each block.

2.3 Quantum-Safe Zero-Knowledge Proofs

In cryptography, zero-knowledge proof (ZKP) [8] is a method by which one party (i.e., a prover) can prove to another party (i.e., a verifier) that a given statement is true, without disclosing additional information beyond the fact that the statement is true. ZKPs need to satisfy the formal requirements of *completeness*, *soundness*, and *zero-knowledge*, thereby enabling one to build trustless applications. Earlier design of ZKPs are not quantum-resistant and those that only use collision-resistant hash functions are plausibly post-quantum secure. **Z**ero-**K**nowledge **S**calable **T**ransparent **AR**gument of **K**nowledge (zk-STARK) [1] and MPC-in-the-Head (MPCitH) [10] are well-known quantum-safe ZKP examples widely used in practice.

2.4 zk-Rollups

A zero-knowledge rollup (a.k.a. zk-Rollup) [18] is a Layer-2 scaling technique for Ethereum. zk-Rollups bundle transactions into batches that are executed off-chain and verified on-chain using non-interactive ZKPs, thereby greatly increasing transaction throughput and reducing transaction costs. In practice, zk-Rollups inherit the security of a Layer-1 blockchain and rely on it for data availability and settlement. zk-Rollups are typically realized using two smart contracts deployed on a Layer-1 blockchain, namely a *main contract* and a *verifier contract*. While the main contract stores rollup blocks, track transactions, and monitor state updates, the verifier contract verifies ZKPs submitted by the Layer-2 rollup nodes. When combining zk-Rollups with post-quantum signatures, an off-chain node can verify multiple signatures and generate a (succinct) zero-knowledge proof that could be verified by a smart contract. Such a combination is able to improve the system scalability and user experience significantly.

3 Migration Approaches

To protect Ethereum transactions from potential risks of the rapid growth of quantum computing, we describe two incremental proposals for migrating Ethereum towards post-quantum security in this section. Without loss of generality, legacy transactions will be used as examples throughout this section.

3.1   Layer-1 Hard Fork

Our first proposal is to introduce new transaction types that augments each exist-ing transaction type with a new parameter **proofUri**. This parameter contains the URI of a quantum-safe zero-knowledge proof (e.g., zkSTARK or MPCitH). With the introduction of **proofUri**, an augmented legacy transaction will be processed as illustrated in Fig. 2.

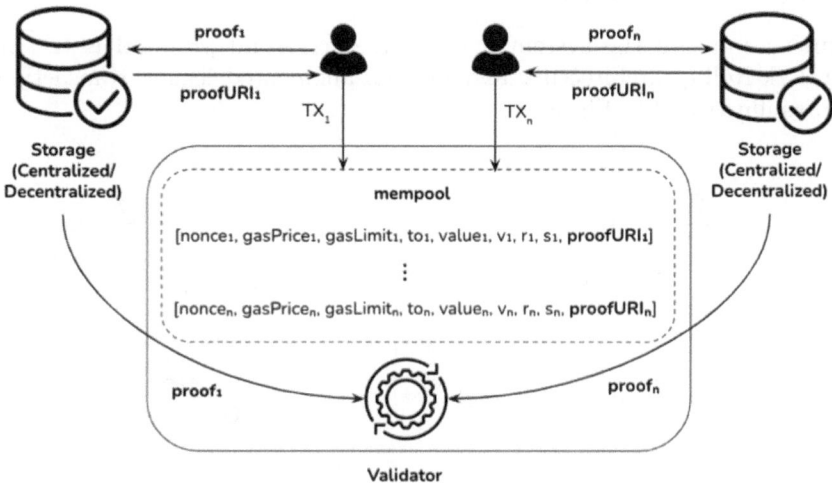

Fig. 2. The Process of Augmented Legacy Transactions

- A user generates a post-quantum secure zero-knowledge proof for the state-ment that he/she knows a secret (e.g., a mnemonic phrase) which can be used to generate the user's Ethereum wallet address by following a specified address derivation process (e.g. BIP-39 [14]).
- The user stores the generated **proof** to a selected storage provider and obtains a publicly accessible URI **proofUri**.
- The user creates a transaction by augmenting a legacy transaction with **proo-fUri** and sends it to the mempool of a validator.
- Upon receiving a new transaction in the mempool, a validator first verifies the ECDSA signature in the transaction, followed by retrieving the **proof** from the storage provider with **proofUri** and verifying its validity. A transaction is considered as valid if both signature and proof verification succeed, besides other sanity checks.

The validation of a newly proposed block works as before, except that a validator needs to verify the **proof** retrieved from storage provider with the **proofUri** for each transaction in the block. Note that each transaction is publicly verifiable provided that the corresponding **proof** is publicly available and a user might choose to delete the **proof** after the transaction passes the Ethereum's PoS consensus process. The introduction of **proofUri** does not incur significant storage overhead for existing Ethereum validators and the length of **proofUri** can be further restricted (e.g., less than 256 characters). The computational cost of verifying a **proof** depends on the usage of a specific post-quantum secure zero-knowledge proof scheme.

3.2   Layer-2 zk-Rollups

To further improve the system scalability, our second proposal is to employ Layer-2 zk-Rollup architecture and process augmented legacy transactions in batch, as illustrated in Fig. 3.

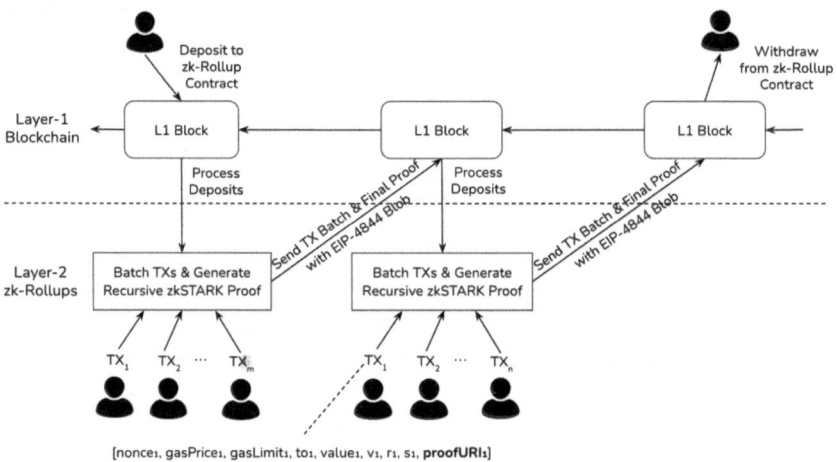

Fig. 3. Scalable Process of Augmented Legacy Transactions with zk-Rollups

The above process follows a typical zk-Rollup workflow with the following modifications:

Given a transaction batch processed by a rollup node, it needs to first retrieve all the zkSTARK proofs using the corresponding **proofUri**'s and then aggregate those proofs into a final proof in a recursive manner.

– The transaction batch together with the single final proof are submitted to the Layer-1 blockchain via a blob transaction as specified by EIP-4844 [4].

To generate a final proof in a recursive manner, the rollup node can leverage a tree-based recursive proof aggregation process as shown in Fig. 4.

During the aggregation process, all the zkSTARK proofs (i.e., $\mathbf{proof}_1, \ldots,$ $\mathbf{proof}_m$) generated by users become the leaf nodes of an aggregation tree. For

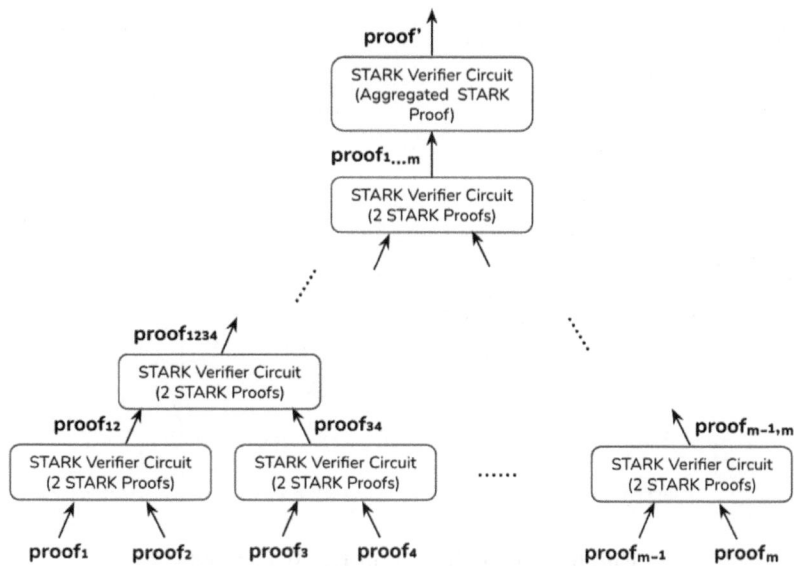

Fig. 4. A Tree-Based Recursive Aggregation of zkSTARK Proofs

each intermediate node, a **STARK** verification circuit is instantiated to aggregate two proofs generated by its child nodes, respectively. Once the aggregated proof (i.e., **proof**$_{1,...,m}$) is generated, another **STARK** verification circuit is employed to compress the aggregated proof into a final proof that can be verified on-chain[2].

3.3 Implementation Considerations

In this subsection, we discuss implementation considerations when deploying the proposed solution in practice.

User Proof Generation. A majority of Ethereum wallets implement the advanced form of deterministic wallet (i.e., Mnemonic code based hierarchical deterministic (HD) wallet) as specified in BIP-32 [20], BIP-39 [14] and BIP-44 [13]. The key derivation in HD wallet follows a tree-like structure in which a parent key can derive a sequence of child keys and each child key can derive a sequence of grandchild keys, as illustrated in Fig. 5.

Hundreds of hash function operations need to be performed for deriving an Ethereum address from a 12/18/24-word's mnemonic code. As a result, proving the statement that a user knows the mnemonic code corresponding to an Ethereum address leads to a complex ZK circuit and long proof generation time.

---

[2] See https://github.com/starkware-libs/starkex-contracts/blob/master/evm-verifier/solidity/contracts/StarkVerifier.sol for an example of a STARK proof verifier written in `Solidity`.

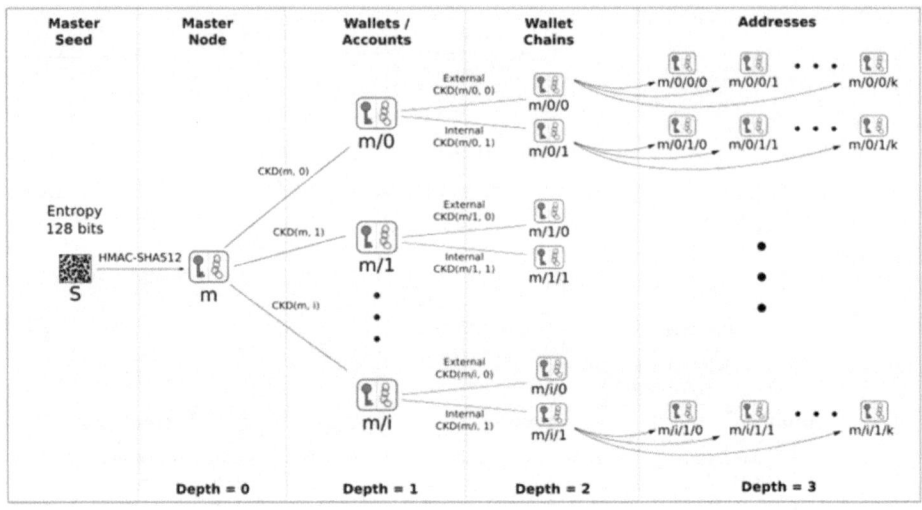

Fig. 5. Key Derivation in HD Wallets [20]

In fact, one can make a flexible trade-off between security and complexity of a proving circuit. For instance, a user may prove that he/she knows the pre-image[3] of the last hash function during the key derivation process in lieu of the knowledge of the mnemonic code itself, which is going to reduce the complexity of a proving circuit significantly.

Mnemonic Code Access. Our proposals require access of a user's mnemonic code in order to generate zero-knowledge proofs. One approach is to ask a user to type the mnemonic code each time he/she would like to send a transaction. However, this approach results in poor user experience. Another approach relies on the secure hardware backed Ethereum wallets (e.g., hardware wallets, mobile wallets, etc.). In this case, a user can choose to store the mnemonic code in the secure hardware and enforce a stringent access policy for accessing it.

Data Availability. The new transaction type introduces the parameter **proofUri** that is used to locate a user generated **proof** off-chain. Both **proofUris** and **proofs** should be held by validators until the finality is reached on Ethereum. After that **proofUri** and **proof** can be safely removed by the validators and users, respectively. This approach does not incur additional overhead with respect to the on-chain storage. Furthermore, it allows users to choose any off-chain (centralized/decentralized) storage provider for storing generated **proofs**.

---

[3] The user can use the mnemonic code and follow the key derivation process as specified in BIP-32 to obtain the pre-image of the last hash function.

Backward-Compatibility and Fallback. Our proposals can achieve backward-compatibility by only introducing minimal changes to the existing implementations of Ethereum validators and clients. Moreover, if an Ethereum wallet does not upgrade to support the new transaction type, it can still submit transactions that only contain ECDSA signatures. However, it is up to an Ethereum validator to determine whether those transactions are still being supported. Such a fallback feature allows Ethereum validators and clients to complete software upgrades in an asynchronous manner.

4   Performance Evaluation

In this section, the preliminary performance evaluation results are presented, followed by a discussion of potential improvements.

4.1   Evaluation Setup

We proceeded to implement the proof generation algorithms as described in Sect. 3.1 based on the following setup:

- **Platform.** We use a standard F32s v2 (Azure) x64 architecture with 32 vCPUs and 64GB RAM running Ubuntu 22.04 LTS.
- **zkVMs.** The Zero-knowledge proof circuits will be generated using zero-knowledge Virtual machines (zkVMs). We use both SP1[4] version 1.0.8-testnet, as well as RISC0[5] version 1.0.1 for proof circuit generation and execution.
- **Proof Algorithm.** The algorithm chosen is described in Eq. 1.

$$\begin{aligned} Sign_q(M, \rho) &= secp256k1(M, Hash(\rho)) \\ Hash(\rho) &= SHA256(\rho) \\ M &= 256 \text{ bit value} \\ \rho &= 256 \text{ bit value} \end{aligned} \tag{1}$$

4.2   Evaluation Benchmarks

Table 1 shows the results of execution of proof generation for a target security of 100 bits.

The proof size generated per signature is at least 5 MBytes of data which is not gas-efficient as expected. Proof generation also takes several minutes on a CPU which is not feasible for most end-user transactional activities. Allocating more memory to the virtual machines does not improve the performance.

We next explored the possibility of reducing the size of the proof based on:

1. *Adjusting the security bits.* This adjustment is supported on the SP1 zkVM and the results are shown in Table 2.

---

[4] available at https://github.com/succinctlabs/sp1.

[5] available at https://github.com/risc0/risc0.

Table 1. Comparing SP1 and RISC0 proof generation

zkVM	SP1	RISC0
Proof Size (Bytes)	5,333,944	28,675,808
Memory Consumed (MBytes)	42,350	8,470
Program CPU Cycles	10,552,692	13,631,488
Execution Time (seconds)	309	442

Table 2. Comparing Proof Sizes based on Security Bits

Security Bits	60	80	100	128
Proof Size (Bytes)	3,253,624	4,293,784	5,333,944	6,790,168
Memory Consumed (MBytes)	42,350	42,230	42,350	42,150
Execution Time (seconds)	304	304	309	304

The size of proofs generated are linearly reduced based on the security bits, although the memory consumed or execution time remains constant. The reduction of security bits below 100 is not recommended since it will weaken the proof, and allow attackers to potentially use Grover's [9] algorithm, a brute-force search quantum algorithm with quadratic performance speedup, to compromise the system.

2. *Using Layer-2 zk-Rollups as described in Sect.* 3.2. A feature of the zkSTARK proof system is the ability to batch multiple proofs into a constant-size recursive proof. We tested this setup using both SP1 (compressed) and RISC0 (succinct) options to apply to batch 3 proofs and 10 proofs for comparison purposes. We had to increase the platform's memory from 64 GB to 256 GB to accommodate the execution, and retained the original security bit setting of 100. The results of execution are found in Table 3.

Table 3. Comparing Performance of Recusive proofs.

zkVM	SP1		RISC0	
# of proofs combined	3	10	3	10
Recursive Proof Size (Bytes)	1,771,102	1,771,917	1,799,632	1,831,696
Memory Consumed (MBytes)	55,660	96,685	8,428	8,430
Execution Time (seconds)	442	797	982	1974

Based on our results, we can see that by batching the proofs, we can reduce the unit size per proof in exchange for a higher execution time. When using SP0 to batch 10 proofs, the average proof size per proof is reduced to 177 KBytes and execution time per proof is 80 s which starts to become practical.

4.3   Evaluation Discussion

From our preliminary benchmarks, we have obtained some concrete evaluation results which demonstrate a path to practical implementation of our design. The key observations are summarized below.

– The proof generation with SP1 and RISC0 is slow on CPU, thereby limiting their usage in mobile and desktop wallet applications directly. A dedicated ZKP proving service with hardware acceleration (e.g., GPU, FPGA, etc.) should be deployed to improve user experience in practice, as illustrated in Fig. 6. Note that the ZK proving service should run inside a trusted execution environment (TEE) to ensure security of processing users' mnemonic codes. A hardware-based remote attestation process [6] is conducted each time a mobile or desktop wallet needs to connect to the proving service for generating a ZK proof. Although such an implementation increases the attack surface area, it will improve usability and user adoption.

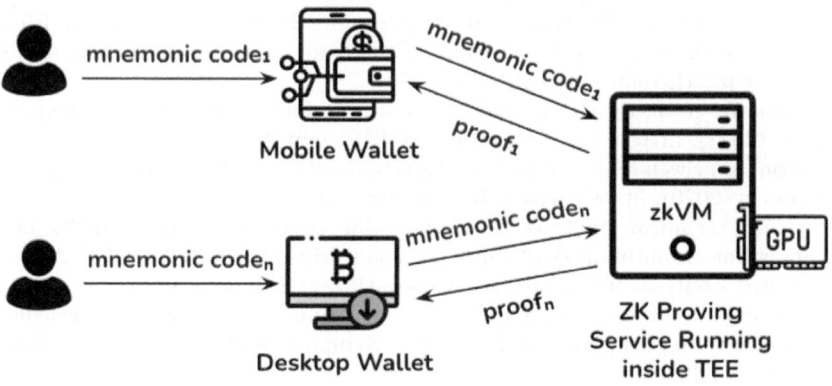

Fig. 6. A ZK Proving Service Running inside a Trusted Execution Environment (TEE)

– The proof size of zkSTARK is large and using a data availability solution like EIP-4844 [4] can effectively reduce the cost of storing transaction batches and the corresponding aggregated proofs on chain.
– The proof aggregation can effectively amortize the proof size, at the cost of higher proof generation time and hardware platform requirements.

5   Conclusion

Although the threat of quantum computers to endanger the security of Ethereum may be some years away, the early articulation of clear requirements and direction of how a quantum-safe Ethereum can be achieved will remove any wild speculation to the fate of Ethereum and its community. We have proposed concrete approaches that focused on backward-compatibility for a smooth post-quantum migration experience for both users and developers, while not compromising on quantum-safety. The initial performance evaluation demonstrates the technical viability of our solution, and highlights the need for proof generation time and proof size reduction in order to make the solution usable. As our future work, we will focus on continuing improving performance and user experience of our solution by exploring memory-efficient ZK proof systems as well as customized ZK circuits.

References

1. Ben-Sasson, E., Bentov, I., Horesh, Y., Riabzev, M.: Scalable, transparent, and post-quantum secure computational integrity. Cryptology ePrint Archive, Paper 2018/046 (2018). https://eprint.iacr.org/2018/046
2. Buterin, V.: How to hard-fork to save most users' funds in a quantum emergency. Technical report. (2024). https://ethresear.ch/t/how-to-hard-fork-to-save-most-users-funds-in-a-quantum-emergency/18901
3. Buterin, V., Conner, E., Dudley, R., Slipper, M., Norden, I., Bakhta, A.: Eip-1559: fee market change for eth 1.0 chain. Ethereum improvement proposals (2019). https://eips.ethereum.org/EIPS/eip-1559
4. Buterin, V., et al.: Eip-4844: Shard blob transactions. Ethereum improvement proposals (2022). https://eips.ethereum.org/EIPS/eip-4844
5. Buterin, V., Swende, M.: Eip-2930: Optional access lists. Ethereum improvement proposals (2020). https://eips.ethereum.org/EIPS/eip-2930
6. CCC: A technical analysis of confidential computing v1.3 (2022). https://confidentialcomputing.io/wp-content/uploads/sites/10/2023/03/CCC-A-Technical-Analysis-of-Confidential-Computing-v1.3_unlocked.pdf
7. Giacomelli, I., Madsen, J., Orlandi, C.: {ZKBoo}: faster {Zero-Knowledge} for boolean circuits. In: 25th Usenix Security Symposium (Usenix Security 2016), pp. 1069–1083 (2016)
8. Goldwasser, S., Micali, S., Rackoff, C.: The knowledge complexity of interactive proof-systems. In: Proceedings of the Seventeenth Annual ACM Symposium on Theory of Computing, STOC '85, pp. 291–304. Association for Computing Machinery, New York (1985). https://doi.org/10.1145/22145.22178
9. Grover, L.K.: Quantum mechanics helps in searching for a needle in a haystack. Phys. Rev. Lett. **79**(2), 325 (1997)
10. Ishai, Y., Kushilevitz, E., Ostrovsky, R., Sahai, A.: Zero-knowledge from secure multiparty computation. In: Proceedings of the Thirty-Ninth Annual ACM Symposium on Theory of Computing, STOC '07, pp. 21–30. Association for Computing Machinery, New York (2007). https://doi.org/10.1145/1250790.1250794
11. Kuo, P.C., Cheng, C.M., Tam, C.: Eip-7592: precompile for falcon signature verification. Ethereum improvement proposals (2023). https://github.com/ethereum/EIPs/pull/8103/files
12. NIST: Post-quantum cryptography (2017). https://csrc.nist.gov/projects/post-quantum-cryptography
13. Palatinus, M., Rusnak, P.: Multi-account hierarchy for deterministic wallets. Bitcoin improvement proposals (2014). https://github.com/bitcoin/bips/blob/master/bip-0044.mediawiki

14. Palatinus, M., Rusnak, P., Voisine, A., Bowe, S.: Mnemonic code for generating deterministic keys. Bitcoin improvement proposals (2013). https://github.com/bitcoin/bips/blob/master/bip-0039.mediawiki
15. Shor, P.W.: Polynomial-time algorithms for prime factorization and discrete logarithms on a quantum computer. SIAM J. Comput. **26**(5), 1484–1509 (1997). https://doi.org/10.1137/S0097539795293172
16. Tan, T.G., Zhou, J.: Layering quantum-resistance into classical digital signature algorithms. In: Liu, J.K., Katsikas, S., Meng, W., Susilo, W., Intan, R. (eds.) ISC 2021. LNCS, vol. 13118, pp. 26–41. Springer, Cham (2021). https://doi.org/10.1007/978-3-030-91356-4_2
17. Tan, T.G., Zhou, J.: Migrating blockchains away from ECDSA for post-quantum security: a study of impact on users and applications. In: Garcia-Alfaro, J., Navarro-Arribas, G., Dragoni, N. (eds.) DPM CBT 2022. LNCS, pp. 308–316. Springer, Cham (2023). https://doi.org/10.1007/978-3-031-25734-6_19
18. Thibault, L.T., Sarry, T., Hafid, A.S.: Blockchain scaling using rollups: a comprehensive survey. IEEE Access **10**, 93039–93054 (2022)
19. Unruh, D.: Computationally binding quantum commitments. In: Fischlin, M., Coron, J.-S. (eds.) EUROCRYPT 2016. LNCS, vol. 9666, pp. 497–527. Springer, Heidelberg (2016). https://doi.org/10.1007/978-3-662-49896-5_18
20. Wuille, P.: Hierarchical deterministic wallets. Bitcoin improvement proposals (2012). https://github.com/bitcoin/bips/blob/master/bip-0032.mediawiki
21. Zoltu, M.: Eip-2718: typed transaction envelope. Ethereum improvement proposals (2020). https://eips.ethereum.org/EIPS/eip-2718

Accelerating Blockchain Application Development: Integrating Blockchain as a Service Within Low-Code Platforms

Sheng He[1,2(✉)] ⓘ, Qinglin Huang[1,2], Shaoshuai Jiao[1,2], Zepeng Lin[1,2], Jinxuan Lin[1,2], Jun Ren[1,2], Dengbin Xiong[1,2], and Liang-Jie Zhang[3(✉)] ⓘ

[1] National Engineering Research Center for Supporting Software of Enterprise Internet Services, Shenzhen 518057, China
heshengpku@gmail.com
[2] Kingdee Research, Kingdee International Software Group Co., Ltd., Shenzhen 518057, China
[3] College of Computer Science and Software Engineering, Shenzhen University, Shenzhen 518060, China
zhanglj@szu.edu.cn

Abstract. The integration of Blockchain as a Service (BaaS) within the Low-Code Development Platforms (LCDPs) is expected to revolutionize the speed and accessibility of blockchain application development. This paper explores the synergy between BaaS and the low-code or no-code development environments in Platform as a Service (PaaS) frameworks, examining opportunities, challenges, and implications for developers and organizations. LCDPs have gained popularity for simplifying application creation, empowering a broad spectrum of developers from citizen developers to experienced professionals. Concurrently, blockchain technology offers enhanced security and transparency but traditionally requires specialized skills for implementation. By embedding BaaS capabilities within LCDPs, developers can leverage blockchain benefits without extensive expertise, streamlining development processes and accelerating time-to-market for blockchain applications. Additionally, it addresses challenges related to security, scalability, and the complexity of managing blockchain operations within simplified development environments. By presenting best practices and identifying opportunities, this paper aims to contribute to the advancement of accessible and efficient blockchain application development.

Keywords: Blockchain as a Service · Low-Code Development Platform · Platform as a Service · Decentralized Application

1 Introduction

Blockchain technology is a revolutionary innovation [1] that offers exceptional security, transparency, and decentralization, with the potential to transform industries such as finance and supply chain management (SCM) [2]. However,

J. Feng et al. (Eds.): ICBC 2024, LNCS 15425, pp. 16–32, 2025.
https://doi.org/10.1007/978-3-031-77095-1_2

its adoption in enterprises has been slowed by the complexity of deployment and the need for specialized expertise. Blockchain as a Service (BaaS) addresses these challenges by providing cloud-based solutions [3] that simplify blockchain development, making it accessible to a broader range of developers [4]. BaaS platforms streamline infrastructure management, smart contract development, and application integration, enabling users to deploy blockchain solutions without deep technical knowledge.

Low-Code Development Platforms (LCDPs) [5] further democratize software development by allowing users to build applications through visual, drag-and-drop interfaces [6]. Integrating BaaS with LCDPs creates a synergy that accelerates blockchain application development, enabling a wide range of developers, from beginners to experts, to leverage blockchain without needing specialized knowledge of its complexities. This integration simplifies the development process, reduces time-to-market, and promotes wider adoption of blockchain technology across industries with a blockchain-based micro-services architecture [7].

This paper explores the integration of BaaS within LCDPs, focusing on the technical and practical aspects of this approach within Platform as a Service (PaaS) frameworks. Section 2 examines the challenges in blockchain application development, identifying the barriers to adoption. Section 3 provides a framework for integrating BaaS with LCDPs and outlines the key functionalities such as smart contract deployment and decentralized data management. Section 4 discusses the development process in the low-code platforms for blockchain applications, including rapid deployment and management. Section 5 presents a real-world use case in SCM, demonstrating the benefits of integrating BaaS with LCDPs. Section 6 concludes with insights and future research directions, highlighting the potential for further innovations in accessible blockchain application development.

2   Challenges in Blockchain Application Developments

While blockchain technology offers transformative potential across various industries [8], its widespread adoption is constrained by several technical and operational challenges. The complexities of blockchain application development include technical barriers, resource demands, scalability limitations, security risks, and regulatory challenges. We also evaluate how current BaaS offerings from leading providers mitigate these challenges and their potential integration with low-code development methodologies.

2.1   Technical Complexities

Developing blockchain applications presents inherent complexities due to the need for expertise in various blockchain protocols, robust smart contract development, and decentralized network management:

- *Understanding Blockchain Protocols*: Blockchain systems rely on sophisticated cryptographic protocols and consensus mechanisms, such as Proof of

Work (PoW), Proof of Stake (PoS), and Practical Byzantine Fault Tolerance (PBFT). Developers must deeply understand these protocols to design blockchain applications that capture core attributes, such as immutability, decentralization, and transparency [9].

– *Smart Contract Development*: Smart contracts are self-executing agreements with terms directly written into code. Their development requires proficiency in programming languages such as Solidity for Ethereum and a thorough understanding of potential vulnerabilities such as reentrancy attacks. Ensuring that smart contracts are secure, efficient, and free from bugs is crucial, as errors can result in irreversible consequences [10].

– *Managing Decentralized Networks*: Blockchain applications often operate on decentralized networks, where data is distributed across multiple nodes. Managing these networks involves maintaining synchronization, achieving consensus, and handling node failures [11]. The complexity of managing decentralized networks increases with the scale and geographic distribution of the network, posing significant challenges for developers [12].

The development of blockchain applications requires a specialized skill set, including knowledge of cryptography, distributed computing, and programming languages tailored to blockchain platforms. The scarcity of skilled blockchain developers exacerbates these challenges, often leading to higher development costs and extended project timelines. Furthermore, the rapid evolution of blockchain technologies necessitates continuous learning and adaptation, increasing the resource demands on organizations.

Scalability remains one of the most significant challenges in blockchain development [13]. The trade-off between decentralization and scalability, often referred to as the "blockchain trilemma", forces developers to balance security, decentralization, and performance. For instance, while Bitcoin and Ethereum are highly secure and decentralized, they suffer from low throughput and high latency, making them less suitable for high-frequency transactional applications in enterprises.

2.2 Security Risks and Compliance Challenges

Security is a critical concern in blockchain development due to the sensitive and high-value nature of the data involved [14]. Blockchain's transparency and immutability can impede the protection of personal information, particularly under regulations such as the General Data Protection Regulation (GDPR), which emphasizes data control and the right to be forgotten. Smart contracts are also prone to coding vulnerabilities that can lead to significant financial losses, as seen in several high-profile cases. Furthermore, private key management is hard, while losing a private key can result in the permanent loss of access to blockchain assets.

Blockchain operates within a complex and evolving regulatory environment [15], with different countries enforcing diverse rules on data privacy, financial transactions, and anti-money laundering. For developers and organizations, navigating these regulations is challenging, as non-compliance can lead to legal consequences and fines. Additionally, the decentralized nature of blockchain complicates compliance with traditional regulations, which are typically designed for centralized systems.

2.3   Evaluation of Existing BaaS Offerings

Several cloud service providers offer BaaS solutions to simplify blockchain development by providing pre-configured environments, tools, and services that abstract much of the underlying complexity [16].

IBM Blockchain[1] focuses on enterprise-grade blockchain solutions with robust support for *Hyperledger Fabric*, emphasizing security, scalability, and regulatory compliance. **Amazon Managed Blockchain**[2] provides tools for creating and managing scalable blockchain networks using popular frameworks such as *Ethereum* and *Hyperledger Fabric*, with an emphasis on ease of deployment and integration with other AWS services. **Ant Blockchain**[3] supports multiple blockchain engines, including *Hyperledger Fabric, enterprise Ethereum Quorum,* and *Ant Blockchain*, enabling users to build stable and secure production-level blockchain environments while simplifying deployment, operation, and management challenges. **Tencent Cloud BaaS**[4] integrates blockchain engines such as *ChainMaker* and *Hyperledger Fabric*, supporting various deployment forms such as public, private, and hybrid clouds, and provides a full lifecycle of visual operation capabilities, enabling users to quickly deploy and scale blockchain applications.

These BaaS platforms vary in their approach to blockchain, offering different levels of customization, security features, and support for various blockchain protocols. By combining the user-friendly nature of low-code or no-code platforms with the flexibility of BaaS [17], organizations can overcome many of the challenges associated with blockchain development.

3   Integrating BaaS Within LCDP

In enterprise applications, consortium blockchains demand higher standards for maintenance, security, and compliance than public blockchains. When combined with LCDPs, BaaS streamlines the development process, allowing for the rapid creation and deployment of blockchain applications. This includes managing blockchain nodes for network stability, providing templates for smart contract creation, and integrating blockchain functions into existing applications, along with additional features such as data storage and distributed identity management. Figure 1 presents the technical framework for integrating BaaS with LCDPs, highlighting the key components that enable this integration.

---

[1] https://www.ibm.com/blockchain.
[2] https://aws.amazon.com/managed-blockchain.
[3] https://antdigital.com/products/baas.
[4] https://cloud.tencent.com/product/tbaas.

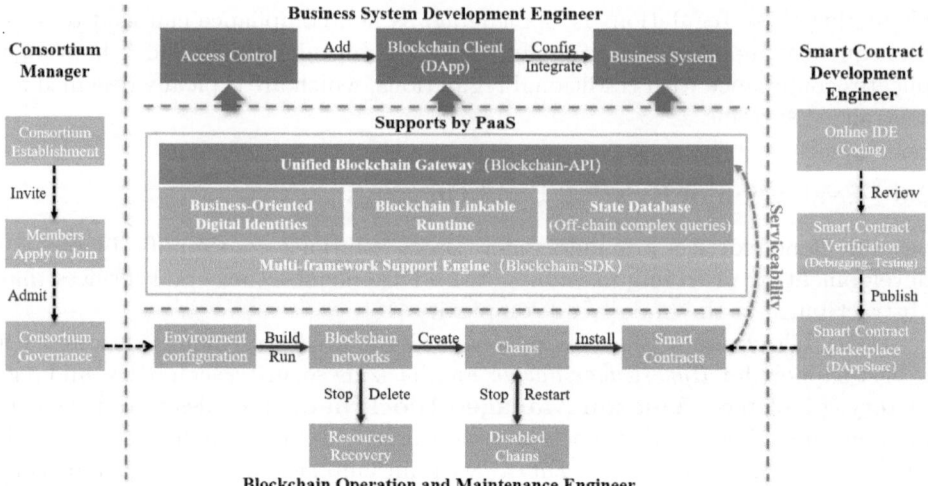

Fig. 1. The blockchain integration framework within LCDPs offers a key feature: the serviceability of smart contracts. This involves encapsulating the deployment, invocation, monitoring, and management of smart contracts into standardized services. These services are then made accessible to developers through APIs or other service-oriented interfaces, simplifying the use and administration of smart contracts.

3.1   Blockchain Integration Framework

The "blockchain console" is a graphical user interface designed to integrate core BaaS functionalities into PaaS environments, prioritizing user experience and accessibility. It enables users to quickly set up blockchain networks, manage nodes, deploy smart contracts, and monitor network activities through an intuitive interface. The console's key strengths include (1) quick setup, which minimizes the time and expertise needed for deployment; (2) flexible management tools that simplify operations for users of all technical levels; and (3) a scenario-oriented design that supports a variety of applications, from commercial and private deployments to proof-of-concept projects.

The blockchain console simplifies blockchain operations and lowers the entry barrier for non-professional developers by providing a "one-stop" user experience. It enables various roles within an organization to interact with blockchain technology efficiently, streamlining processes from network setup to smart contract management. Users are categorized into four key roles:

1. **Consortium Manager**, who oversees consortium creation, member invitations, and application certification, forming the business ecosystem of the consortium blockchain.
2. **Blockchain Operation and Maintenance Engineer**, responsible for configuring the environment, building the network, and managing smart contract deployment and maintenance.

3. **Smart Contract Development Engineer**, who uses an online integrated development environment (IDE) to code, test, and publish smart contracts in a marketplace.
4. **Business System Development Engineer**, who integrates blockchain services into business systems via a unified blockchain gateway.

The unified blockchain gateway, built on the serviceability of smart contracts, streamlines integration and enhances the user experience by offering standardized services for smart contract management. The console's unified approach allows different roles to collaborate seamlessly, enhancing the overall efficiency of blockchain implementation within the organization. For example, the flexible management capabilities empower operation and maintenance engineers to easily adjust network resources, while developers can focus on creating and refining smart contracts without needing deep technical expertise in blockchain infrastructure.

3.2   Functionalities for Foundational Users

Consortium Management. Consortium blockchains, designed as collaborative multi-organization frameworks, aim to enhance the efficiency, security, and transparency of business processes. Effective management is critical to the success of a consortium blockchain, relying on well-defined processes and protocols to foster cooperation and trust among participating members. The blockchain console offers a comprehensive suite of tools for consortium management, enabling managers and members to oversee and collaborate within the network efficiently.

The consortium manager plays a pivotal role in the establishment and ongoing operation of the consortium. Responsibilities include creating the blockchain consortium, setting foundational parameters such as membership criteria, consensus mechanisms, node permissions, and data privacy policies, as well as inviting and evaluating potential new members. Additionally, managers are tasked with removing non-compliant members to maintain the integrity and efficiency of the consortium.

Once admitted, consortium members engage in network operations, including node management, participation in consensus processes, and deployment of smart contracts. Depending on the consortium's governance protocols, members can access and share blockchain data, thereby facilitating synchronization and collaboration across organizations.

Blockchain Infrastructure Management. A robust blockchain development environment must support a wide range of underlying technologies to meet diverse development needs. The multi-framework support integrates various block-chain frameworks, such as *Hyperledger Fabric*[5], *FISCO BCOS*[6], and

---

[5] https://www.hyperledger.org/projects/fabric.
[6] https://www.fisco-bcos.org.

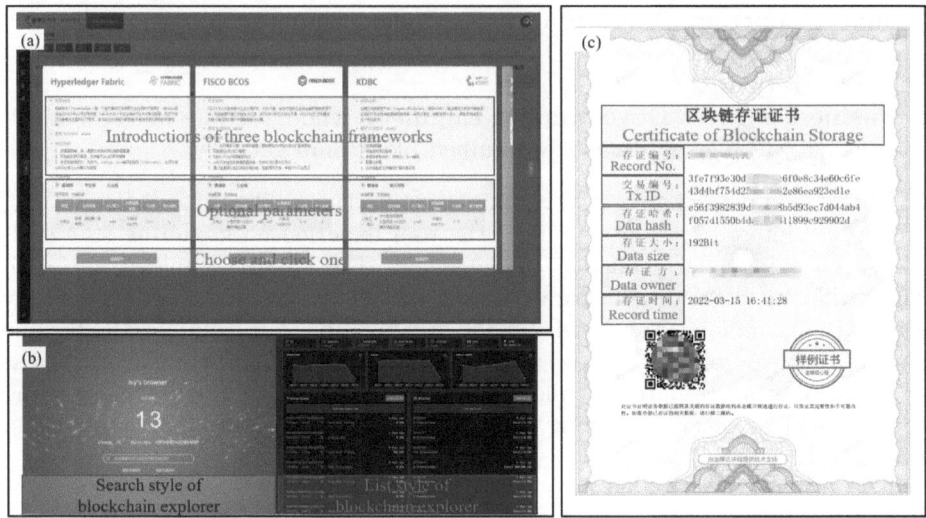

Fig. 2. This figure showcases three key product functionalities, including (a) the multi-framework support, (b) customizable blockchain explorers in two styles, and (c) an example certificate verifying successful data recording on the blockchain.

custom enterprise solutions as shown in Fig. 2(a), providing developers with the flexibility to select the most appropriate framework for their specific projects.

The console allows the simultaneous operation of multiple networks and chains, each functioning independently to avoid cross-network interference. Additionally, it supports cross-chain services, enabling the transfer of assets and information between different blockchains within the ecosystem, thus fostering interconnected systems that enhance overall functionality. This multi-chain architecture increases system flexibility and scalability, ensuring stable and efficient blockchain operations.

The graphical user interface simplifies the management of blockchain infrastructure, allowing users to perform actions such as adding, building, running, stopping, restarting, and deleting networks. This user-friendly approach reduces technical complexities and lowers barriers to blockchain adoption.

Blockchain Network Creation and Operation. Within the blockchain console, developers can configure key parameters for blockchain networks, including node count, consensus mechanisms, encryption standards, and programming languages for smart contracts. Tools for real-time monitoring and management provide insights into critical metrics such as block height and transaction counts.

The console facilitates the deployment of blockchain networks across diverse geographic locations, enabling the creation of distributed, highly available networks that support business continuity and operational stability.

By leveraging cloud-native tools such as Kubernetes and Docker, the blockchain console allows for deployment across multiple cloud providers, enhancing network autonomy, flexibility, and disaster recovery capabilities. The console also supports the integration of external business partners into the blockchain network through authorized interfaces, promoting cross-organizational collaboration and innovation.

3.3   Functionalities for Application Users

State Database and Blockchain Explorer. Efficient data querying and analysis are essential for blockchain applications. Traditional blockchain frameworks typically rely on key-value (KV) storage, which can restrict the ability to perform complex queries. The state database addresses this limitation by synchronizing the latest state and historical transactions on the blockchain, thereby supporting complex queries and improving data retrieval efficiency.

The state database updates in real time as new blocks are added, accurately reflecting the latest changes in transactions and account statuses. A customizable blockchain explorer as illustrated in Fig. 2(b) allows users to tailor the interface and functionality to their specific needs, providing real-time updates and detailed data visualization that enhance user interaction and data analysis capabilities.

Smart Contract Deployment. Smart contracts are integral to blockchain technology, enabling automated, rule-based transactions. The online Integrated Development Environment (IDE) within the blockchain console supports the entire lifecycle of smart contract development, including coding, testing, and deployment directly within a web browser.

The online IDE offers advanced features such as debugging, project management, and security testing, allowing developers to concentrate on contract logic without being encumbered by infrastructure complexities.

Moreover, the blockchain console features a smart contract marketplace where developers can share, sell, and deploy smart contracts. This platform promotes contract reuse, reduces development costs, and accelerates the pace of blockchain innovation.

Access Control and System Monitoring. Robust access control and comprehensive system monitoring are critical for safeguarding sensitive data and ensuring the security of enterprise-grade blockchain applications. A detailed permission management system enables users to request and manage access to specific blockchain networks, while administrators can enforce granular access controls based on factors such as interface type, access frequency, and authorization duration.

Multi-dimensional monitoring tools offer a real-time overview of the network's health, tracking key performance indicators such as transaction rates, response times, and success rates. These tools facilitate the prompt identification and resolution of potential issues, thereby maintaining the stability and security of the blockchain network.

4   Blockchain Application Development Process

Developing blockchain applications within enterprises requires a strategic app-roach to identifying specific scenarios where blockchain technology adds substan-tial value. This section outlines practical steps for developing blockchain appli-cations using LCDPs, discusses workflows for integrating blockchain functionali-ties, and provides examples to support blockchain application development. It also explores methods for simplifying smart contract creation, managing decentralized data, and addressing common challenges in blockchain application development.

4.1   Assessing Blockchain Application Value

Blockchain enhances trust, security, and transparency through decentralized data storage and smart contract automation. Before developing blockchain appli-cations, enterprises must evaluate whether blockchain is suitable for their specific scenarios:

- **Self-Proof**: By allowing enterprises to self-verify the authenticity and integrity of their operations, blockchain reduces reliance on third-party audits and streamlines compliance processes.
- **Transaction Trust**: Blockchain fosters trusted transactions by providing an immutable, shared source of truth that enhances trust among business partners, suppliers, and customers.
- **Data Assetization**: The ability to turn data into verifiable assets introduces new mechanisms for data validation and transaction, reducing the costs and time associated with traditional verification methods.

The immutable and transparent nature of blockchain directly impacts enterprise decision-making, operational efficiency, and compliance management. These attributes make blockchain particularly valuable in scenarios requiring high levels of trust.

4.2   Decentralized Application Modes

Storage Applications. Blockchain technology provides a secure method for storing and verifying data, ensuring its integrity, authenticity, and immutability. This application mode is well-established and widely used in industries with stringent data security requirements, such as finance.

Financial Industry: Blockchain offers a robust solution for recording and veri-fying financial data, including accounting records and transaction histories. Its immutability ensures that data, once recorded, cannot be altered, thus enhancing the credibility and transparency of financial reports, simplifying audits, reducing costs, and fostering confidence among investors and regulators.

Traceability Applications. Blockchain enables enterprises to trace and doc-ument the entire lifecycle of products, from production to consumption. By recording each stage on the blockchain, these applications provide a transparent, immutable record of the movement of goods, thereby enhancing trust and authenticity.

Product Authentication: Blockchain prevents counterfeiting by securely recording critical information, such as production details, transportation routes, and sales data. This ensures that product information is tamper-proof, allowing consumers and regulators to verify the origin and authenticity of products in real time, which enhances brand trust and product quality.

Shared Applications. Shared blockchain applications utilize distributed ledgers and smart contracts to facilitate data and process sharing across multiple stakeholders. These applications can be categorized into process-based and data-based sharing.

Contract Management: Blockchain automates contract execution through smart contracts, reducing default risks and enhancing transparency. Automation minimizes human errors, disputes, and compliance risks, thereby improving the efficiency of contract management.

Credit Services: Blockchain offers financial institutions reliable tools for credit assessment by securely storing and sharing transaction histories. This enables more accurate and efficient credit evaluations, reduces credit risk, and fosters trust.

Transactional Applications. Transactional applications leverage blockchain to facilitate asset transfers, verify transactions, and immutably record them. These applications are divided into core-oriented and peer-to-peer transactions.

Core-Oriented Transactions: In sectors such as tax administration, blockchain can issue unique electronic invoices, automate verification processes, and track transactions, thereby enhancing tax compliance and reducing fraud.

Peer-to-Peer Transactions: In supply chain finance, blockchain improves transparency and trust by tracking goods flow and automating contract terms. This accelerates fund flows, reduces costs, and mitigates risks associated with traditional transaction models.

4.3   Development Process Using LCDPs

Blockchain applications are reshaping traditional business models by offering secure, transparent, and efficient transactional environments. As blockchain technology advances, its applications are anticipated to permeate additional industries, driving digital transformation. Practical steps for developing blockchain applications using LCDPs include:

1. *Defining Requirements:* Clearly outline the business requirements and identify the specific blockchain functionalities needed.

2. *Platform Selection:* Select an appropriate LCDP that supports blockchain integration, taking into account factors such as ease of use, scalability, and the range of supported blockchain frameworks.
3. *Workflow Design:* Design workflows that integrate blockchain functionalities, including setting up the blockchain network, configuring nodes, deploying smart contracts, and managing data flows.
4. *Testing and Deployment:* Utilize platform tools to rigorously test the application in a controlled environment before deploying it into production.

Smart contracts are essential for automating blockchain transactions, and LCDPs enhance this process through online IDEs, which facilitate coding, testing, and deployment. Developers can utilize code libraries and marketplaces within these platforms to accelerate development and ensure adherence to industry standards. To further strengthen smart contract robustness, automated security testing tools are vital for detecting and mitigating vulnerabilities before deployment, thereby improving the overall security of blockchain applications.

Efficient data partitioning techniques are necessary to distribute data across nodes effectively, which helps maintain system performance and meets legal requirements. Additionally, integrating blockchain applications with external databases enables off-chain storage of large datasets, keeping on-chain data manageable and optimizing overall system performance. Continuous monitoring tools are critical for maintaining data integrity and system health, allowing the platform to manage the complexity and scale of decentralized data environments effectively.

Scalability issues can be mitigated by optimizing node configurations and implementing advanced consensus mechanisms, which enhance the network's ability to handle increased loads. Security involves deploying robust encryption protocols, multi-factor authentication, and continuous monitoring strategies to protect against potential threats. Interoperability requires designing applications that can seamlessly interface with existing systems and external blockchains through standardized solutions, ensuring smooth integration across diverse technological environments.

5 Use Case Study in SCM

SCM is a highly promising area for blockchain applications due to the inherent complexities of modern supply chains, which involve numerous stakeholders, extensive documentation, and a critical need for transparency and security. This section explores the role of blockchain in SCM, identifies specific challenges it addresses, and provides a detailed guide for implementing blockchain-based SCM solutions using LCDPs.

5.1 Role of Blockchain

Blockchain technology significantly enhances SCM by providing a decentralized and immutable ledger for recording transactions and tracking goods. The key advantage lies in its ability to provide a shared, tamper-proof record accessible to all participants in the supply chain, thereby enhancing trust, reducing fraud, and eliminating the need for intermediaries. This ledger documents every step in the supply chain, enabling real-time tracking of goods from origin to destination, while cryptographic mechanisms protect data from unauthorized access and tampering.

Supply chains face challenges such as complex coordination among stakeholders, limited visibility, and the need for rapid verification of goods. Blockchain addresses these issues by creating a unified source of truth that streamlines coordination between manufacturers, suppliers, logistics providers, and retailers. Its immutability guarantees that data entries are accurate and verifiable, which reduces the time and costs of product authentication. Moreover, the auditability of blockchain records ensures compliance with industry regulations and standards, making it an effective tool for managing complex supply chain processes.

5.2   Implementing Blockchain-Based SCM Solutions Using LCDPs

LCDPs simplify the creation of blockchain-based SCM solutions by providing pre-built components and user-friendly interfaces, enabling developers to concentrate on business logic rather than technical complexities. Below is a structured approach for implementing a blockchain-based SCM solution:

1. **Define Supply Chain Processes and Requirements**: Identify key supply chain processes that will benefit from blockchain, such as order tracking, inventory management, and product verification. Clearly define objectives for integration, including enhancing transparency, reducing fraud, and improving transaction speed.
2. **Select an Appropriate Low-Code or No-Code Platform**: Choose a platform that supports blockchain integration, scalability, and robust security. Ensure compatibility with existing enterprise systems, such as ERP and CRM, to facilitate a cohesive workflow.
3. **Design and Configure the Blockchain Network**: Set up the blockchain network by configuring nodes, selecting an appropriate consensus mechanism, and defining access controls to secure permissions. Develop smart contracts to automate critical SCM transactions, including order execution, payment processing, and compliance verification.
4. **Implement Traceability and Data Management**: Enable real-time tracking of goods using blockchain features, allowing stakeholders to monitor product movements throughout the supply chain. Utilize decentralized data storage solutions to ensure that only authorized parties have access to sensitive data.
5. **Test and Deploy the Solution**: Conduct comprehensive testing to ensure that the blockchain solution meets all functional and security requirements. Deploy the solution across the supply chain and provide training for stakeholders to ensure effective adoption and use.

6. **Monitor and Optimize**: Continuously monitor the blockchain network using performance tracking tools, making adjustments as necessary to maintain optimal operation. Collect feedback from stakeholders and implement iterative improvements to enhance system efficiency and address new challenges as they arise.

5.3   Distributed Digital Identity Management

Blockchain-based digital identities, unlike traditional ones, are virtual representations of individuals or entities. These identities consist of data and attributes that enable secure verification. Linked to public and private keys, they facilitate secure transaction signing and proof of ownership.

BaaS offerings within LCDPs provide standardized services to create, manage, and utilize digital identities for individuals, businesses, and other entities. These identities are crucial for verifying transactions, accessing services, and executing smart contracts within blockchain networks. They connect business systems to blockchain networks with customizable configurations tailored to specific needs, enhancing security and efficiency in supply chain operations.

Individual Digital Identities represent stakeholders, such as suppliers and logistics providers, incorporating unique identifiers like usernames or blockchain addresses. Authentication methods include passwords, digital signatures, or biometric data.

Organizational Digital Identities are vital for enterprise-level SCM applications. Defined by unique identifiers, such as organization names or blockchain addresses, these identities authenticate organizational roles within the blockchain network.

Lifecycle management includes the creation, maintenance, renewal, and deactivation of digital identities, each associated with specific roles within the blockchain network, establishing access rules and data ownership policies. Effective management ensures that only authorized users or organizations can access the network, enhancing security and trust within the supply chain.

5.4   Implementation of Data Storage Applications

The "one-click record-to-chain" feature streamlines recording data or assets on the blockchain, allowing users to perform blockchain transactions with ease. This process includes data encryption, block packaging, and verification through consensus mechanisms, ensuring security and immutability. Once recorded, on-chain data cannot be altered and is accessible for verification, enabling its use as legal evidence.

Key functionalities of data storage applications include defining data storage entities, mapping business relevance, managing running tasks, recording logs, and handling storage schemes and certificates:

Data Storage Entities are fundamental data units in blockchain data storage applications, crucial for mapping, storing, and managing data on the blockchain. Users can customize the structure of these entities to meet specific business needs, defining fields such as name, type, and description. Blockchain synchronization ensures real-time data consistency across business systems, streamlining operations such as creation, updating, querying, and deletion, and improving efficiency in data management.

Business Relevance Mapping links storage entities with real-world business objects, ensuring stored data accurately reflects business operations. Users can define relationships between entities and business processes, such as production, logistics, or transactions, providing a comprehensive view of the data lifecycle. LCDPs support field-level association mapping, aligning data with business logic, which is essential for applications such as contract management and financial operations.

Running Tasks convert business data into block-chain recorded data, customizable by format, content, frequency, and blockchain entry conditions. Scheduled tasks handle regular updates such as financial reporting, while event-triggered tasks respond to specific actions such as contract signing. Batch tasks allow simultaneous recording of multiple data sets, boosting efficiency. Customizing task management enables businesses to align blockchain processes with operational needs.

Recorded Logs document all blockchain operations, which are generated automatically to capture real-time changes whenever data is added to the blockchain, allowing users to verify data consistency and integrity. Field-level verification further ensures accuracy, making recorded logs vital for auditing and validating blockchain-stored data.

Storage Schemes provide customizable processes for recording data on the blockchain, tailored to specific business needs. Standard templates are available for common use cases, enabling quick deployment and resource savings. Users can define data collection, verification, and storage protocols, as well as set rules for running tasks, allowing flexible management across different scenarios.

Certificates are the primary output of blockchain storage services, serving as formal proof that data has been successfully recorded on the blockchain. As an example shown in Fig. 2(c), certificates contain details such as data content, recording time, and data hash, to verify authenticity and integrity. Certificates can be customized to align with business branding and standards, and the straightforward generation process facilitates their use in legal and business contexts, such as contract verification and legal disputes.

5.5 Blockchain-Enabled Ecological SCM Use Case

A process flow for an ecological SCM system using blockchain is outlined below (see Fig. 3). We systematically implemented a proof of concept (PoC) within LCDPs for this business process to validate its feasibility and effectiveness:

1. *Supplier Onboarding*: Prospective suppliers register on the blockchain network by establishing digital identities. Rigorous vetting verifies credentials and certifications, which are then encoded into smart contracts representing supplier profiles, terms, and service agreements.

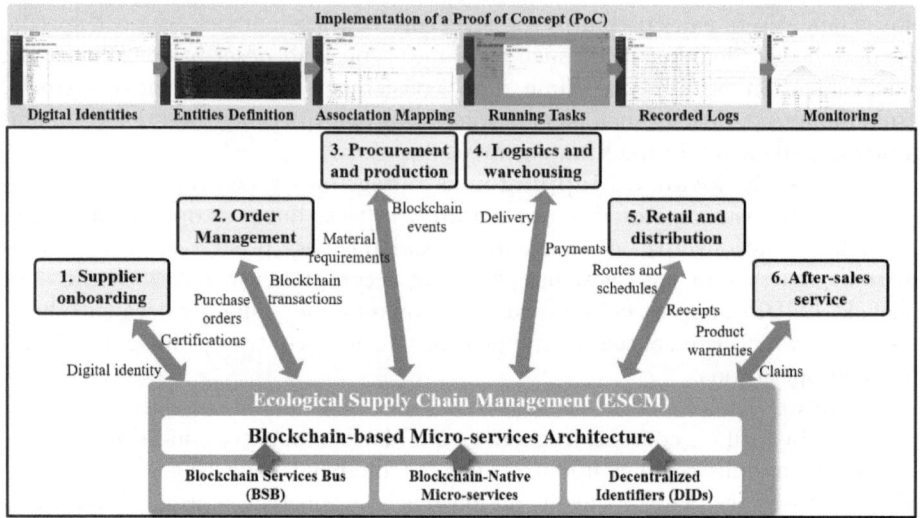

Fig. 3. A systematic implementation of a proof of concept (PoC) for the business process of ecological SCM.

2. *Order Management*: Purchase orders are initiated as blockchain transactions referencing product catalogs. Smart contract logic validates these orders against inventory levels, logistics capacity, and supplier profiles. Once validated, orders are immutably recorded on the shared ledger.
3. *Procurement and Production*: Suppliers receive notifications of purchase orders and material requirements through blockchain events. Manufacturers update production schedules and inventory levels on the blockchain. Smart contracts automate just-in-time purchasing based on demand forecasts and inventory data.
4. *Logistics and Warehousing*: Sensors on containers transmit location and condition data throughout transit. Smart contracts trigger automated payments or other actions upon verified proof of delivery or other milestones. Distributed warehouse management coordinates inventory flows and signals availability.
5. *Retail and Distribution*: Retailers access blockchain records to check inventory availability. Delivery routing and scheduling are optimized based on demand analysis. Payments are automatically processed upon verified receipt of goods via blockchain transactions.
6. *After-sales Service*: Product warranty details are immutably registered on the blockchain, ensuring integrity and traceability. Customers can initiate warranty claims through blockchain transactions, which activate smart contract protocols to verify terms and trigger settlements or repairs.

This blockchain-based SCM solution enhances transparency, automation, provenance, and resilience across ecological supply chains. It demonstrates the integration process from design to deployment, showcasing improvements in traceability, transparency, and efficiency. The implementation also offers insights into best practices and lessons learned, providing a framework for further applications in ecological SCM.

6   Conclusion and Future Work

This paper examines the integration of Blockchain as a Service (BaaS) within Low-Code Development Platform (LCDPs), highlighting its potential to simplify and accelerate blockchain application development. Embedding BaaS capabilities within LCDPs significantly reduces development complexity and time, making blockchain accessible to a wider range of developers, from novices to experts. This approach offers key benefits such as faster development cycles, enhanced security through a distributed immutable ledger, and broader accessibility. However, challenges remain, including the need to ensure security and scalability within simplified development environments and to provide robust management tools for handling blockchain network complexities.

To maximize the benefits of integrating BaaS within LCDPs, developers and organizations should adopt best practices for blockchain and low-code development, prioritize scalable solutions to support growth, and invest in training to equip teams with the necessary skills. Future research should focus on enhancing security and privacy measures tailored to low-code blockchain environments, optimizing performance for large-scale applications, and exploring cross-platform integration to expand the versatility of these technologies. As BaaS and LCDPs continue to evolve, their convergence could democratize blockchain development, fostering innovation, wider adoption of decentralized applications (DApps), and advancements in digital trust and transparency across industries.

Acknowledgments. This work is supported by the Shenzhen Science and Technology Program (Grant No. KJZD20231023094501003), the National Key R&D Program of China (Grant No. 2023YFB3308502), and the Key-Area R&D Program of Guangdong Province, China (Grant No. 2020B0101090003). The authors would like to express our sincere gratitude to Dr. Huan Chen and Dr. Jing Zeng for their insightful discussions and invaluable assistance.

References

1. Zhang, L.J., et al.: BCOA: blockchain open architecture. In: Xu, C., Xia, Y., Zhang, Y., Zhang, L.J. (eds.) ICWS 2021. LNCS, vol. 12994, pp. 90–111. Springer, Cham (2022). https://doi.org/10.1007/978-3-030-96140-4_7
2. Wamba, S.F., Queiroz, M.M.: Blockchain in the operations and supply chain management: benefits, challenges and future research opportunities. Int. J. Inf. Manage. **52**, 102064 (2020). https://doi.org/10.1016/j.ijinfomgt.2019.102064
3. Chen, H., Zhang, L.J.: FBaaS: functional blockchain as a service. In Chen, S., Wang, H., Zhang, L.J. (eds.) ICBC 2018. LNCS, vol. 10974, pp. 243–250. Springer, Cham (2018). https://doi.org/10.1007/978-3-319-94478-4_17

4. Zheng, W., et al.: NutBaaS: a blockchain-as-a-service platform. IEEE Access **7**, 134422–134433 (2019). https://doi.org/10.1109/ACCESS.2019.2941905
5. Sahay, A., et al.: Supporting the understanding and comparison of low-code development platforms. In 2020 46th Euromicro Conference on Software Engineering and Advanced Applications (SEAA), pp. 171–178. IEEE, August 2020. https://doi.org/10.1109/SEAA51224.2020.00036
6. Tharani, J.S., Zelenyanszki, D., Muthukkumarasamy, V.: A UI/UX evaluation framework for blockchain-based applications. In: Chen, S., Shyamasundar, R.K., Zhang, L.J. (eds.) ICBC 2022. LNCS, vol. 13733, pp 48–60. Springer, Cham (2022). https://doi.org/10.1007/978-3-031-23495-8_4
7. He, S., et al.: A blockchain-based micro-services architecture for distributed business. In: Wang, Q., Feng, J., Zhang, L.J. (eds.) ICBC 2023. LNCS, vol. 14206, pp. 38–53. Springer, Cham (2023). https://doi.org/10.1007/978-3-031-44920-8_3
8. Zhang, L.J.: MRA: metaverse reference architecture. In: Tekinerdogan, B., Wang, Y., Zhang, L.J. (eds.) ICIOT 2021. LNCS, vol. 12993, pp. 102–120. Springer, Cham (2022). https://doi.org/10.1007/978-3-030-96068-1_8
9. He, S., et al.: Layered consensus mechanism in consortium blockchain for enterprise services. In: Joshi, J., Nepal, S., Zhang, Q., Zhang, L.J. (eds.) ICBC 2019. LNCS, vol. 11521, pp. 49–64. Springer, Cham (2019). https://doi.org/10.1007/978-3-030-23404-1_4
10. Zheng, Z., et al.: An overview on smart contracts: challenges, advances and platforms. Futur. Gener. Comput. Syst. **105**, 475–491 (2020). https://doi.org/10.1016/j.future.2019.12.019
11. Li, C., Zhang, L.J.: A blockchain based new secure multi-layer network model for Internet of Things. In: Proceedings of 2017 IEEE International Congress on Internet of Things (ICIOT), pp. 33–41. IEEE (2017). https://doi.org/10.1109/IEEE.ICIOT.2017.34
12. He, S., Xing, C., Zhang, L.J.: A business-oriented schema for blockchain network operation. In: Chen, S., Wang, H., Zhang, LJ. (eds.) ICBC 2018. LNCS, vol. 10974, pp. 277–284. Springer, Cham (2018). https://doi.org/10.1007/978-3-319-94478-4_21
13. Khan, D., Jung, L.T., Hashmani, M.A.: Systematic literature review of challenges in blockchain scalability. Appl. Sci. **11**(20), 9372 (2021). https://doi.org/10.3390/app11209372
14. Leng, J., Zhou, M., Zhao, J.L., Huang, Y., Bian, Y.: Blockchain security: a survey of techniques and research directions. IEEE Trans. Serv. Comput. **15**(4), 2490–2510 (2020). https://doi.org/10.1109/TSC.2020.3038641
15. Buterin, V., et al.: Blockchain privacy and regulatory compliance: towards a practical equilibrium. Blockchain Res. Appl. **5**(1), 100176 (2024). https://doi.org/10.1016/j.bcra.2023.100176
16. Singh, J., Michels, J.D.: Blockchain as a service (BaaS): providers and trust. In: 2018 IEEE European Symposium on Security and Privacy Workshops (EuroS&PW), pp. 67–74. IEEE, April 2018. https://doi.org/10.1109/EuroSPW.2018.00015
17. Curty, S., Härer, F., Fill, H.G.: Design of blockchain-based applications using model-driven engineering and low-code/no-code platforms: a structured literature review. Softw. Syst. Model. **22**(6), 1857–1895 (2023). https://doi.org/10.1007/s10270-023-01109-1

Legacy Compatible and Sybil Resistant Decentralized Identity Management for IoTs

Songlin He[1,2(✉)], Xukang Lyu[3], and Dongliang Chu[3]

[1] Southwest Jiaotong University, Chengdu 610031, Sichuan, China
[2] Manufacturing Industry Chain Collaboration and Information Support Technology Key Laboratory of Sichuan Province, SWJTU, Chengdu 610031, Sichuan, China
sohe@swjtu.edu.cn
[3] Zhejiang New Rise Digital Technology Co., Ltd., Hangzhou 311899, China
{clu,chudongliang}@newrisedt.com

Abstract. With the exorbitant growth of Internet of Things (IoTs) scale and the interconnections among such a vast realm of heterogeneous objects, it is vital to uniquely identify the IoT devices and build a robust identity management (IdM) system, thus enabling many desired security mechanisms including authentication, authorization and secure exchange. An appealing technology to overcome the shortcomings of conventional online identity models and empower the construction of a robust IoT IdM system lies in decentralized identity, also known as *self-sovereign* identity. The existing literature on IoT IdM systems omits several critical functionalities like legacy compatibility and consideration of the IoT device lifecycle. In this study, we tackle these issues and present DIdM-IoT, a system for realizing secure and robust decentralized identity management in the IoT setting. We elaborate on the system details and give security sketch. Experimental results demonstrate its effectiveness and efficiency.

Keywords: IoT · Decentralized identity management · Blockchain · Legacy compatibility · Sybil resistance · Decentralized storage

1 Introduction

The Internet of Things (IoTs) aiming at connecting everything (e.g., individuals, organizations and smart devices) is omnipresent in our daily lives and reckon as the fundamental supporting pillar for the development of various application scenes such as healthcare, smart cities or mobility services [6,15–17,21,27,39]. However, the exorbitant growth of the number of IoT devices and their interconnections via Internet expose large attack surface, making them attractive targets for cyber-attackers. The solution to manage such a vast realm of interconnected heterogeneous objects lies in uniquely identifying these devices and furthermore building a robust identity management (IdM) system, referring to

J. Feng et al. (Eds.): ICBC 2024, LNCS 15425, pp. 33–49, 2025.
https://doi.org/10.1007/978-3-031-77095-1_3

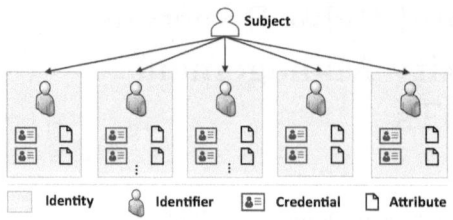

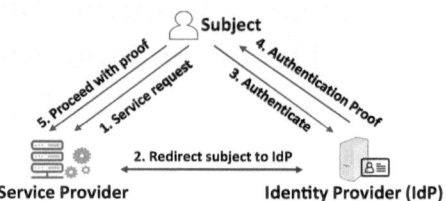

Fig. 1. The relationship between various terminologies.

Fig. 2. The conventional IdM system model.

the process of representing and recognizing entities as digital identities in virtual networks [2,5,11,21,27]. It is foreseeable that the unique digital identities supported by a robust IdM system would facilitate the connection or communication among billions of IoT devices and their potential millions of users, upon which many desired security mechanisms including authentication, authorization or secure exchange can be constructed.

In an IdM system, a *subject* (e.g., a person in physical world) can possess different *identities* for different contexts (e.g., studying in school as a student or interacting with a bank as a consumer). Each identity is identified by an *identifier* (e.g., a student ID or an email address) in a specific context and consists of multiple *attributes* (e.g., name and age). An attribute used for authentication can be a *credential* (e.g., certificate, password, fingerprint and etc.), and similarly each identity may own multiple credentials. The relationship between subjects, identities, identifiers, attributes, and credentials is depicted in Fig. 1. Typically, an IdM system model consists of three stakeholders: a subject (usually known as a user), an identity provider (IdP) and a service provider. Figure 2 shows an exemplary instance of conventional online IdM system where the subject who requests the services from a service provider would be redirected and challenged by an IdP about the subject's identity via an authentication protocol.

The online IdM model has evolved through critical stages including *isolated*, *federated*, *centralized* and *user-centric* models during the past three decades. However, these legacy online identity management systems are not capable of fulfilling the requirements for building the robust IdM system in the IoT setting, largely due to that: Firstly, the existing online IdM systems are built around third-party IdPs, which is easy to be a target for cyber criminals and pose a single point of failure [40]. Secondly, the existing online IdM models are mainly people-oriented. For instance, emails or social platform IDs are ubiquitously used for identifying persons [24]. However, the IoT devices usually may not be suitable to equip with these identifiers. Thirdly, a variety of IoT manufactures and systems featuring proprietary IdM solutions and distinct communication protocols coexist, leading to application silos and hindrance of interoperability [11,21]. Fourthly, the IoT devices need to go through a serials of stages during its lifetime such as getting sold, decommissioned or compromised [20]. However, these legacy online IdM models are not inherently designed for the IoT setting and therefore lack of a holistic design thinking regarding the whole lifecycle identity management for the IoT devices and their various attributes. One promising technology to overcome the above challenges resides in the *decentralized identity* (or interchangeably known as *self-sovereign identity* (SSI)) [7], as specified by initiatives such as Decentralized Identity Foundation [9] and Decentralized Identifiers (DID) working group of World Wide Web Consortium (W3C) [31]. However, there still exist some challenges to be tackled, as evidenced by the insufficiencies of existing decentralized identity based methods [5, 11, 21, 23, 27, 35, 36, 40]. Specifically, we highlight the following three aspects.

- **Sybil Resistance**. If an IoT device or its owner can obtain numerous fake identities and therefore gain disproportionately large impact on the network, the basic requirement of unique identification or further functionalities such as accountability cannot be realized.
- **Legacy Compatibility**. A straightforward way of issuing identity and credentials for IoT devices requires proactive participation of IoT service providers to digitally sign and act as the identity issuer. However, a *chicken-and-egg* problem may arise: the IoT service providers may not be willing to become the proactive issuer unless they see a flourishing of the decentralized identity-enabled IoT IdM ecosystem; on the flip side, such an ecosystem cannot boom without active participation of these existing IoT service providers. Essentially this predicament is a *bootstrapping* problem though in reality there exist rich legacy data on IoT device providers' web services.
- **IoT Device Lifecycle**. The IoT IdM system should cover the entire lifecycle regarding an IoT device such as being manufactured, deployed, repaired, upgraded, resold or eventually retired. This requires comprehensive decentralized identity based operations, e.g., identity registration, identity retrieval, identity updating, and identity revocation. Apart from identity-related operations, another challenge pertinent to IoT device lifecycle is the robust storage of device relationships [20], e.g., deployed-by, upgraded-by or repaired-by, which would empower better IoT device management such as accountability or predictive maintenance.

Contributions. Overall we propose a decentralized identity management system dubbed DIdM-IoT for the IoT setting and our contributions can be summarized as follows.

- We realize legacy compatible credential issuance for IoT devices based on oracle protocols and sybil-resistant identity in the sense of being unique per subject and per IoT device.
- A method for managing the full lifecycle of IoT devices is presented, which relies on blockchain for secure management.
- The proposed system is analyzed to show that it satisfies the design goals. We also implement and evaluate the key component of the system, and the experimental results show its practicality and efficiency.

2   Background

2.1   Decentralized Identity and Main Components

The decentralized identity (*a.k.a.* self-sovereign identity) is a new online IdM paradigm that enables entities to have real ownership of their identity information and control the usage of these information. Usually decentralized identity contains the following fundamental components:

Claim. A claim$_i$ is a statement about an entity. Each claim contains an attribute a_i and a value v_i, i.e., claim$_i = \{a_i, v_i\}$. E.g., a_i is a string "name" while v_i is a string "Cindy".

Decentralized Identifier (DID). A DID is a string for uniquely identifying a party in the landscape of decentralized identity. For example,

$$did : DID\_Method : 987654321abcdefghi$$

where did is a fixed prefix, DID_Method is a specific decentralized identity scheme [33], and 987654321abcdefghi is the identifier specified in the DID_Method. Our system supports the usage of DID by hinging on a PKI-like infrastructure like [10,25], which stores the mapping relationship between a DID and the corresponding public key. Hence, the public key and DID of a party can be used interchangeably in the later description.

DID Document Object (DDO). Each DID is associated with a DDO that contains the DID itself, the bound public keys (for authentication or encryption), the service endpoints (e.g., a URL for messaging the entity) and other metadata such as timestamp. A DID can be *resolved* to fetch a DDO via concrete ways that defined in the DID method [32].

Verifiable Credential (VC). We follow the definition of a VC from the W3C Verifiable Credentials specification [34], which states that a VC is a set of claims $\{claim_i\}$ issued by an issuer. The authenticity of these claims is verifiable and therefore, if valid, trustable.

2.2   IoT Device Lifecycle

IoT devices typically need to go through multiple stages during its lifetime where a range of parties including manufacture, supplier, shipper, installer, maintainer, and etc. [12,22] are involved in such a supply chain. As pointed out by Khan *et al.* [20], two main challenges need to be addressed in a secure, efficient and trustworthy fashion for IoT identity and access management: one is to deal with the ownership and identity relationship for IoT devices while the other one lies in the management of attributes and relationships of an IoT device.

Table 1. Comparison with others (✓: Good, *: Medium, ×: Bad, −: Not Specified).

Related Work	Sybil Resistance	Legacy Compatible (Bootstrapping)	Robust Local Management of VCs	IoT Lifecycle
Bouras et al. [5]	*	×	×	*
DIAM-IoT [11]	×	*	×	✓
Luecking et al. [21]	*	×	×	*
CanDID [23]	✓	✓	×	×
DT-SSIM [27]	−	−	✓	*
Weingaertner et al. [35]	✓	×	×	*
SmartDID [36]	✓	×	×	*
BIFIT [40]	*	×	×	*
This Work (DIdM-IoT)	✓	✓	✓	✓

Specifically, IoT device relationships can be categorized as, e.g., *manufactured_by*, *owned_by*, *deployed_by*, *upgraded_by*, *repaired_by*, and *sold_by* and the relationship involves different parties such as *device-to-subject* and *device-to-device*. An IoT IdM system should be capable of robustly record and maintain these information for monitoring, management or realizing accountability. The identity related operations are mainly performed when an IoT device is sold to a customer.

2.3 Oracle Protocols

One key building block to construct our system is *oracle protocols* [13,26,30, 37,38]. An oracle protocol forwards and provides authentic data retrieved from authoritative resources, which are typically TLS-enabled web servers. In particular, an oracle system allows a prover to prove (publicly or to a specific verifier) that some data indeed originate from a certain source, e.g., identified by its TLS certificate. Moreover, the prover can also optionally prove arbitrary statements regarding the data. Two concrete instantiation of oracle protocols enabling privacy-preservation of user data are *Town crier* [37] and *DECO* [38]. These two methods accomplish the similar task (i.e., a prover can convince a verifier that some (possibly private) data retrieved from a source satisfies a specific predicate) while differentiate with underlying implementation where the former relies on secure multi-party computation (MPC) [19] to protect data privacy and authenticity and zero-knowledge proofs (ZKPs) [3] to show the satisfying of the predicate, and the latter hinges on trusted execution environments (TEEs), instantiated by Intel SGX [8], to prove the authenticity of TLS sessions and statements regarding TLS plaintexts [23]. The oracle protocols play a critical role to handle the legacy-compatibility issue: an oracle protocol can take as input the rich online and available data, e.g., the IoT devices' information maintained on manufactures' or retailers' web servers, and generate a proof of authenticity of these information. This whole procedure is agnostic to existing IoT service providers, e.g., IoT manufactures or retailers.

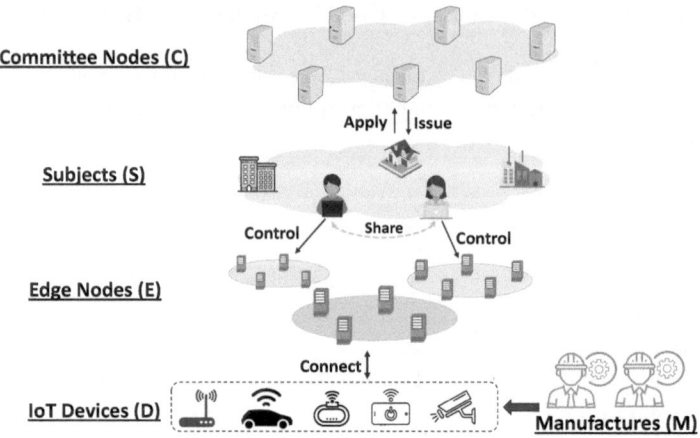

Fig. 3. The system model for decentralized IoT IdM system.

2.4   Decentralized Identity Management System for IoT

There exist a range of literature regarding the construction of decentralized identity management system for IoT setting. We compare with these works and Table 1 summarizes the comparison.

- *Sybil Resistance.* The works [5,11,21,35,40] cannot fully ensure sybil resistance. Specifically, Luecking et al. [21] proposed a trust management framework and the sybil attack is limited by two factors, i.e., the cost of Proof of Work (PoW) of each identity-creation transaction and assigning no trust for newly created identity. However, the sybil attack is still possible if an adversary can benefit more by creating fake identities or a sybil identity is bootstrapped with initial trust by highly trusted identities. Fan et al. [11] did not consider the sybil-resistant issue. Bouras et al. [5] assumes each entity registers to the blockchain network only once, but such an assumption seems impractical and lacks concrete mechanism description. Zhu et al. [40] assign a unique identifier to each appliance by extracting the digital characteristics like power consumption via Discrete Wavelet Transform (DWT). However, there lacks a mechanism to verify the authenticity of such a feature and sybil attack is still possible.
- *Legacy Compatible.* The existing schemes [5,11,21,27,35,36,40] did not consider the problem where either the credential issuance for IoT devices still requires the proactive participation of IoT service providers, or these schemes are unable to fully leverage the rich data from legacy online IoT web services. Meanwhile, the issuer varies in different schemes, e.g., in [21], the credential issuer is the subject itself, while an alternative architecture of issuer is embodied by a decentralized committee [5,36].
- *IoT Lifecycle.* The entire IoT device lifecycle should be considered in an IoT IdM system [20]. Most of existing works [5,21,27,35,36,40] just considered operations in partial phases during the whole IoT device lifecycle.

CanDID [23] is a general platform for decentralized identity and therefore there need proper tuning, e.g., device binding and device relationship management, when adapting to the specific IoT setting.

3 System Model and Design Goals

As depicted in Fig. 3, the decentralized IoT identity management system consists of six types of parties:

- **Committee nodes** C (each denoted by C_i) are entities that follow a *permissioned* model in the sense that participants in C are known to each other when forming such a committee. Practically organizations or companies who are interested in building the ecosystem of the decentralized IoT IdM system can be the committee members. The committee C is mainly responsible for (i) securely storing necessary information; (ii) issuing the decentralized identity and verifiable credentials for system participants.
- **Subjects** S (each denoted by S_i) are entities who own IoT devices. Subjects can be natural persons, organizations, companies, families etc. Subjects are the *centre* of the whole decentralized IoT IdM system.
- **Edge nodes** E (each denoted by E_i) are servers that deployed and controlled by a specific subject S_i. Edge nodes can provide more computation and storage power in comparison with IoT devices (see below) and act as the intermediary layer between subjects and IoT devices.
- **IoT devices** D (each denoted by D_i) are devices, e.g., sensors or actuators, deployed and controlled by subjects featuring limited computation and storage power. These devices are usually connected with a set of edge nodes, which perform the resource intensive tasks and only communicate with IoT devices via simple commands.
- **Manufactures** M (each denoted by M_i) are the manufactures for the IoT devices.
- **Verifiers** V (each denoted by V_i) are entities that can verify the authenticity of decentralized identities or credentials of participants in the system. Any party (e.g., committee nodes, subjects) can be a verifier.

3.1 Threat Model and Considerations

We consider the attacker with the standard abilities that: (i) the utilized cryptographic schemes are secure; (ii) the adversary is considered *static* and is restricted to *probabilistic polynomial time* (P.P.T) algorithms; (iii) the adversary can corrupt up to t (out of n) nodes in the issuer committee C, where $t < \frac{n}{3}$. For a blockchain network, the number of corrupted nodes are upper-bounded by $\frac{1}{3}$; (iv) we consider that the communication channels are *asynchronous*. Nevertheless, for some system components, the communication model requirement may vary, e.g., the different instantiated consensus mechanism in the blockchain network may require *partial synchronous* [4] or can be *asynchronous* [14], and the distributed key generation scheme requires *weak synchrony* for liveness [18]. Besides, we consider that a unique real-world identifier for IoT devices, e.g., serial number, exists on IoT service providers' (e.g., IoT manufactures' or retailers') TLS-enabled websites. In practice, a subject (e.g., a consumer who purchased an IoT device) can see the information (possibly not only serial number but also more information/claims) about the IoT device once sign in the system that IoT service providers provide.

3.2   Design Goals

Security Properties. The DIdM-IoT system aims to satisfy the following security properties:

- **Sybil-resistance**. An adversary can *at most* obtain one unique credential for a controlled subject or IoT device in the decentralized identity landscape.
- **Unforgeability**. An adversary cannot forge the credentials of honest subjects and IoT devices that controlled by honest subjects.
- **Credential validity**. An adversary can obtain credentials of subjects and IoT devices only for real-world identities that subjects and IoT devices own.

Utility Properties. The DIdM-IoT system also aims to meet the following utility properties:

- **Legacy Compatibility**. The IoT IdM system can directly utilize the existing infrastructure instead of relying on the IoT manufactures to proactively join in the system for issuing identities and credentials.
- **Scalability**. The IoT IdM system should be scalable to accommodate an increasingly vast amount of individuals and things.
- **Interoperability**. The IoT IdM system should provide a universal representation of device identity, thus breaking application silos and potentially facilitating device owners to share data with other entities.

4   System Design

4.1   Instantiating Decentralized Identity for Subjects

In the IoT setting, each IoT device is bound with a subject identified by a unique DID. We leverage the CanDID protocol, which serves as an oracle (denoted with $\mathcal{O}^{\mathsf{CanDID}}$), to instantiate the decentralized identity scheme for subjects (also for manufactures). The identity system converts online identity information (e.g., information retrievable in the existing government-endorsed websites) to usable credentials in specific application contexts.

Identity System for Subjects. There are three entities in the identity system: (i) subjects (S), namely the IoT device owners; (ii) committee nodes (C) for issuing credentials for subjects; and (iii) verifiers (V) of credentials. Briefly, the identity subsystem consists of three phases:

- *Legacy identity information to pre-credentials.* Subjects leverage *oracle protocols* [37,38] to port existing identity claims as *pre-credentials*. For example, a subject S_i's claim in the social security administration website is $\mathsf{claim}_i = \{$ "name", "Cindy"$\}$. The claims can be the input of an oracle protocol, which outputs a proof π^{oracle}, typically a signature over a claim and the subject's public key pk^{S_i}, indicating that the claim about the subject S_i indeed originates from a TLS-enabled (therefore trustable) website. A pre-credential PC can be denoted by $\mathsf{PC} = (\mathsf{claim}_i, pk^{S_i}, \pi^{\mathsf{oracle}})$ where the pk^{S_i} is used to defend against replay attacks.
- *Master credential for unique identification.* Each subject is uniquely identified via a master credential. To obtain a master credential, a subject S_i submits a pre-credential PC containing a unique real-life identity claim, e.g., the social security number v_{SSN} or its *commitment*, to the issuer committee, which verifies the oracle proof π^{oracle} and evaluates the output of a distributed pseudorandom function [1], i.e., $\tilde{v} = \mathsf{DPRF}(sk^C, v_{\mathsf{SSN}})$ where sk^C is the secret key jointly maintained by the committee C; if $\tilde{v}$ is contained in a table $\mathsf{IDTable}$ that maintained by each committee member C_i, it means S_i has claimed the master credential so the committee C takes no action; otherwise C jointly signs and issues the master credential to S_i and adds $\tilde{v}$ to $\mathsf{IDTable}$. The execution of $\mathsf{DPRF}(\cdot)$ is via MPC to ensure the privacy against corrupted issuers. A master credential for a subject is in the following form:

$$\mathsf{cred}^{S_i}_{\mathsf{mas}} = \{pk^{S_i}, \text{"master"}, \{\mathsf{claim}_i\}, \{\text{"de"}, \{a_i\}\}, \sigma^C\}$$

where pk^{S_i} is the subject's public key; "master" is a string indicating that it is a master credential; $\{\mathsf{claim}_i\}$ are the real-world claim(s) used to uniquely identify the subject; $\{$ "de", $\{a_i\}\}$ shows the master credential is deduplicated over the attribute a_i, e.g., name or SSN; σ^C is the signature jointly generated by the committee C as a proof of the validity of the issued master credential.
- *Context-based credential for specific usage.* Upon obtaining a unique master credential $\mathsf{cred}^{S_i}_{\mathsf{mas}}$, a subject can apply for a context-specific credential by submitting $(pk^{S_i}_{new}, \mathsf{cred}^{S_i}_{\mathsf{mas}}, \{\mathsf{PC}_{new}\})$ to the issuer committee C where $pk^{S_i}_{new}$ is a new identifier to be used in the specific context (denoted by ctx) and the $\{\mathsf{PC}_{new}\}$ is a set of pre-credentials needed for the new context. Similar to the master credential issuance, each committee member C_i maintains a table $\mathsf{Issued}_{\mathsf{ctx}}$ that records the issued credentials for this context. If pk^{S_i} is not in the set, the committee C would issue the $\mathsf{cred}^{S_i}_{\mathsf{ctx}}$ to the subject and an entry $(pk^{S_i}, pk^{S_i}_{new})$ is added to the table $\mathsf{Issued}_{\mathsf{ctx}}$. A context-specific credential can be denoted as follows:

$$\mathsf{cred}^{S_i}_{\mathsf{ctx}} = \{pk^{S_i}_{new}, \text{"ctx"}, \mathsf{ctx}, \{\mathsf{claim}_i\}, \{\text{"de"}, \{a_i\}\}, \sigma^C\}$$

where different with the master credential, a new identifier $pk_{new}^{S_i}$, a string "ctx" and a unique context identifier ctx are specified. Note that the $\{claim_i\}$ is a set of claims required for the specific context.

Credential Verification. To verify the validity of a subject's credential, a verifier V can check the followings: (i) the credential $cred_{ctx}^{S_i}$ is properly signed (due to the signature σ^C) by committee C; (ii) the opening, if exist, of any commitment of the claim's value is valid; and (iii) the public key attached with the credential is legal, i.e., the public key does not appear in any public legitimate revocation list.

4.2   System Details

The architecture of the proposed DIdM-IoT system is depicted in Fig. 4, and the concrete system design consists of the following four phases.

– **Phase I for Preparation**. In this phase, each party would be setup and the underlying infrastructures are ready to provide services. Specifically,
  - *Issuer committee.* The issuer committee executes a distributed key generation scheme to generate jointly maintained secret keys for threshold signature and distributed pseudorandom function. To robustly store data, we propose that each committee member can create two private *channels* (e.g., via Hyperledger Fabric), where one called MIoTTable is responsible for maintaining the information about manufactures and their manufactured IoT devices, while the other channel called SIoTIDTable is responsible for maintaining the identity relationship between IoT device owner, namely subject, and IoT devices. In the two channels, data are stored in the form of key-value pairs in the state database.
  - *Subjects.* For a subject (such as a consumer or an organization) or an IoT manufacture, the oracle $\mathcal{O}^{CanDID}$ can be invoked so that each subject (or manufacture) obtains a master credential and an IoT context-based credential (i.e., ctx = "IoT").
  - *DID-PK mapping service.* A DID-PK mapping service is initialized so that whenever this service is invoked, it creates a mapping between a decentralized identifier (DID) and a corresponding DDO. Then the DID is returned to the caller while the DDO is stored, usually in a public blockchain-based infrastructure.
  - *Manufactures.* Similar to subjects, manufactures can apply for the master credential and an IoT-context credential. During preparation, once a manufacture M_i obtains its unique IoT-context credential, M_i registers this identity with the committee nodes, each of whom would then update the MIoTTable with the key pk^{M_i} and the value an empty set.
  - *Edge nodes.* A subject can deploy a private blockchain (e.g., via Hyperledger Fabric) on a set of edge nodes, which connect to IoT devices as a distributed architecture of gateway nodes. At the end of this phase, the private channels are initialized.

– **Phase II for Device Binding and Verifiable credential Issuance**. Upon an IoT device is shipped and delivered to a subject, the DIdM-IoT system allows the subject to self-create and bind with the device's identity. This phase operates as follows:

- *Creating DID*. The subject S_i invokes the DID-PK mapping service such that S_i receives a decentralized identifier (denoted by DID^{D_i}) for the IoT device D_i, with a corresponding DDO^{D_i} containing a public key pk^{D_i}.

- *Legacy compatible pre-credential generation*. By invoking an oracle protocol, S_i can generate a pre-credential for an IoT device, namely $PC^{D_i} = (pk^{S_i}, \text{claim}^{D_i}, \pi^{\text{oracle}})$ where pk^{S_i} is the subject's (i.e., the IoT device owner's) public key, $\text{claim}^{D_i} = (a^{D_i}, C_{v^{D_i}})$ is a claim of the IoT device D_i with the attribute a^{D_i} and the commitment $C_{v^{D_i}}$ to the attribute value v^{D_i}, and π^{oracle} is the authenticity proof stating that such a claim is indeed from a TLS-enabled website that an IoT service provider (i.e., a manufacture or a retailer) offers.

- *Device deduplication and binding*. Upon the pre-credential over a unique identifier (i.e., SN^{D_i}) of the IoT device is generated, the subject S_i performs an interactive procedure with the issuer committee C as follows:
  * The subject sends the shares of the unique identifier (denoted by $[SN^{D_i}]$) along with related fields including pk^{S_i}, pk^{M_i}, DID^{D_i}, $\text{cred}_{\text{IoT}}^{S_i}$, PC^{D_i} and other proofs to the committee C.
  * The committee members possess the share $SN_i^{D_i}$, and they jointly execute an MPC protocol to compute the distributed pseudorandom function result of PRF^{D_i} based on $[SN^{D_i}]$. Then each committee node C_i checks the MIoTTable in the private channel, if pk^{M_i} is contained in the key set, and furthermore the values keyed by pk^{M_i} contain PRF^{D_i}, it means that this IoT device has already applied for the credential, C_i then halts with no more actions. Otherwise, C_i (creates an entry keyed by pk^{M_i} if pk^{M_i} is not in the key set and) appends PRF^{D_i} to the value set of pk^{M_i}.
  * The committee C retrieves pk^{D_i} using DID^{D_i} via the DID-PK mapping service and then verifies the IoT-context credential $\text{cred}_{\text{IoT}}^{S_i}$ of the subject, if valid, each committee member C_i checks the key-value pairs in his/her private channel that maintains the SIoTIDTable, if the key-value pair (pk^{S_i}, pk^{D_i}), where pk^{S_i} is associated with the DID in $\text{cred}_{\text{IoT}}^{S_i}$, exists in the SIoTIDTable, C_i aborts without taking any further action. Otherwise, C_i adds (pk^{S_i}, pk^{D_i}) to SIoTIDTable.

- *Device credential issuance*. The committee members utilize the threshold signature to sign and issue the credential of the IoT device $\text{cred}^{D_i} = \{DID^{D_i}, \text{"DIdM-IoT"}, \{\text{claim}\}, \{\text{"deduplicatedOver"}, [\text{"SN"}]\}, \sigma^C\}$ to the S_i where σ^C is the signature generated by the committee members.

– **Phase III for Maintenance**. Once a subject S_i obtains the credential for the IoT device, the credential should be maintained and managed by the subject itself following the self-sovereign property in decentralized IoT IdM system. To this end, we propose that a private blockchain can be created by the subject over a set of servers, namely edge nodes E^{S_i}. The deployment of

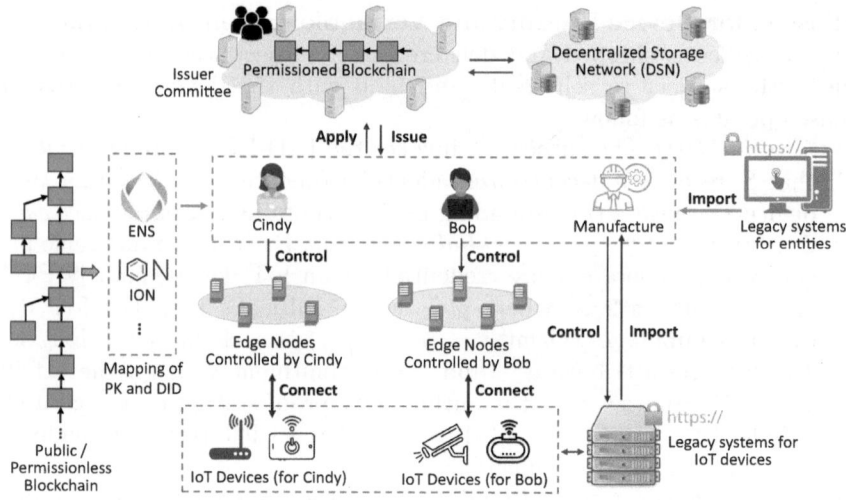

Fig. 4. The system architecture of DIdM-IoT.

edge nodes follows the consideration, i.e., $\mathcal{N}_E^{S_i} \geq 3f_E^{S_i} + 1$ where $\mathcal{N}_E^{S_i}$ is the total number of edges nodes in a private blockchain while $f_E^{S_i}$ is the maximum number of faulty nodes that can be tolerated.

Upon a channel is created in the private blockchain network among edge nodes E^{S_i}, the state database can be initialized where key is DID^{D_i} while the value is a JSON document with the following entries that keyed by: (i) *credential*: the credential $cred^{D_i}$ issued in the last phase for the IoT device D_i; (ii) *manufactured_by*: the IoT manufacture's DID for the device D_i, and the value is "credentialSubject.manufactureDID" in the $cred^{D_i}$; (iii) *owned_by*: the owner's DID of the device D_i, and the value is initialized as the subject's DID; (iv) *deployed_by*: the DID of the party, e.g., the subject, who deployed the device; (v) *upgraded_by*: the DID of the party who upgraded the device; (vi) *repaired_by*: the DID of the party who repaired the device; (vii) *sold_by*: the seller's DID, which can be initialized by the IoT device retailer's DID and can be updated to the subject's DID if the subject resells it. When one of the events above (e.g., upgrading) occurs, the subject S_i is responsible for updating the operator of each event with a timestamp.

– **Phase IV for Revocation.** Once an IoT device retires or the current credential for the IoT device is stolen, S_i can revoke the credential (or possibly apply for a new one). The key idea is that the public key of the revoked credential is appended to a globally public revocation list RL_{IoT}, any IoT device, before interacting with others, would check (via the edge nodes equipping with more computing power) whether the other device appeared in RL_{IoT}.

4.3   Security Sketch

Theorem 1. *Conditioned that the underlying cryptographic primitives are secure, the security of* $\mathcal{O}^{\mathsf{CanDID}}$ *and the considerations hold,* DIdM-IoT *meets sybil-resistance, unforgeability and credential validity against static P.P.T adversary.*

Proof. The sybil resistance property relies on the consideration that each IoT device owns a unique real-world identifier, e.g., serial number SN^{D_i}, and retrievable from IoT service providers' websites. The oracle protocol ensures the integrity of the SN^{D_i} information that sent to the committee C. For committee members, they maintain a table MIoTTable for storing the a set of $(pk^{M_i}, \mathsf{PRF}^{D_i})$ where pk^{M_i} is the manufacture's decentralized identity and PRF^{D_i} is jointly computed by C based on the unique SN^{D_i}. The sybil-resistance guarantee of pk^{M_i} is reduced to the sybil-resistance property in $\mathcal{O}^{\mathsf{CanDID}}$. The unforgeability property is essentially reduced to the security of the threshold signature and the credential validity is reduced to the integrity of the oracle protocols for retrieving the unique identifier and feeding to the committee with validity proof.

Theorem 2. *The* DIdM-IoT *satisfies the legacy compatibility, scalability and interoperability properties.*

Proof. The *legacy compatibility* property is ensured by the oracle protocol, which can export existing data from IoT service providers' TLS-enabled websites without necessitating the proactive involvement of related participants. The *scalability* property indicates that DIdM-IoT can accommodate an increasingly large number of individuals and devices. This is true due to the decentralized architecture of the issuer committee. The *interoperability* is ensured by the decentralized identifier (DID) in the issued credential, which follows the same format/prefix (i.e., "did : DIdM-IoT : IoTDevice456") that pre-agreed by the issuer committee.

5   Experiment and Evaluation

In this section, we present the evaluation of some components in our system, while noting that a full system implementation and evaluation will be our future extension such as the effectiveness and efficiency of DID-PK mapping service instantiated with Microsoft ION [25] and the blockchain network instantiated with Hyperledger Fabric supporting BFT ordering service [29]. Here we evaluate the performance of managing issued credentials via blockchain, specifically about the writing throughput and latency.

The hardware for conducting our experiments is a small-scale cluster of four Virtual Machines (VMs) residing on two heterogeneous servers, representing four nodes to formulate a private blockchain. One server is a Dell PowerEdge R740, which is equipped with 2 Intel(R) Xeon(R) CPU Silver 4114 processors (with 13.75 MB L3 cache and 20 cores of 2.2 GHz for each processor), 256 GB (16 slots × 16 GB/slot) 2400 MHz DDR4 RDIMM memory, and an 8 TB (8 slots × 1TB/slot) 2.5 in. SATA hard drive. The other server is a Dell Precision Rack

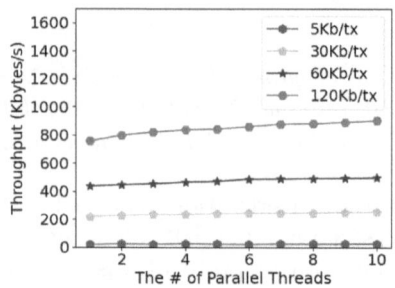
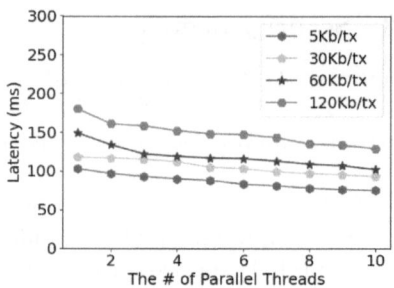

Fig. 5. The throughput of writing IoT verifiable credentials to consortium blockchain channels with various transaction sizes and parallel threads.

Fig. 6. The latency of writing IoT verifiable credentials to consortium blockchain channels with various transaction sizes and parallel threads.

7910, which is equipped with 2 Intel(R) Xeon(R) CPU E5-2630 v3 processors (with 15 MB cache and 6 cores of 2.4 GHz for each processor), 16 GB 2133 MHz DDR4 RDIMM ECC memory, and a 256 GB 2.5 in. SATA solid state drive. The four VMs have the same configuration of 8 vCPUs, 24 GB memory and 800 GB hard drive and are connected via a Local Area Network (LAN). The operating system in each VM is Ubuntu 16.04 (64-bit). The Fabric version is 1.2, the Java version is 1.8.0_211, and the golang version is 1.11.10.

Figures 5 and 6 illustrate the throughput and the latency of writing the issued verifiable IoT credentials to the consortium blockchain (i.e., the private channel with the state database) where the transaction size and the number of writing threads vary in our experiment. The measurements show that the throughput reaches about 900 KBytes/s. We note that for the evaluation of oracle protocols and credential issuance, we refer readers to [28, 37, 38] to perceive an intuitive performance. An interesting future extension lies in implementing a plugin supporting to export pre-credentials from an IoT website.

6   Conclusion

We propose a legacy compatible and sybil resistant decentralized identity management system to tackle the key issues when applying decentralized identity to resolve most of the problems that centralized IdMs pose. Oracle protocols are introduced to bootstrap the IdM ecosystem, and the full lifecycle of IoT devices is considered. Security sketch indicates that the proposed system can ensure needed security properties and the experiment results shows the feasibility and efficiency of the system.

Acknowledgements. This work was supported in part by National Key R&D Project of China (No. 2023YFB3308600). Songlin He is also supported in part by NSFC (No. 62302403), the Fundamental Research Funds for the Central Universities (No. A0920502052301-186).

References

1. Albrecht, M., Grassi, L., Rechberger, C., Roy, A., Tiessen, T.: MiMC: efficient encryption and cryptographic hashing with minimal multiplicative complexity. In: Cheon, J.H., Takagi, T. (eds.) ASIACRYPT 2016. LNCS, vol. 10031, pp. 191–219. Springer, Heidelberg (2016). https://doi.org/10.1007/978-3-662-53887-6_7
2. Babar, S., Mahalle, P., Stango, A., Prasad, N., Prasad, R.: Proposed security model and threat taxonomy for the internet of things (IoT). In: Meghanathan, N., Boumerdassi, S., Chaki, N., Nagamalai, D. (eds.) CNSA 2010. CCIS, vol. 89, pp. 420–429. Springer, Heidelberg (2010). https://doi.org/10.1007/978-3-642-14478-3_42
3. Ben-Sasson, E., Chiesa, A., Tromer, E., Virza, M.: Succinct non-interactive zero knowledge for a von neumann architecture. In: 23rd {USENIX} Security Symposium ({USENIX} Security 2014), pp. 781–796 (2014)
4. Bessani, A., Sousa, J., Alchieri, E.E.: State machine replication for the masses with bft-smart. In: 2014 44th Annual IEEE/IFIP International Conference on Dependable Systems and Networks (DSN), pp. 355–362. IEEE (2014)
5. Bouras, M.A., Lu, Q., Dhelim, S., Ning, H.: A lightweight blockchain-Based IoT identity management approach. Future Internet, 24 (2021)
6. Chen, X., He, S., Sun, L., Zheng, Y., Wu, C.: A survey of consortium blockchain and its applications. Cryptography **8**(2), 12 (2024)
7. Allen, C.: The path to self-sovereign identity. http://www.lifewithalacrity.com/2016/04/the-path-to-self-sovereign-identity.html
8. Costan, V., Devadas, S.: Intel SGX explained. IACR Cryptol. ePrint Arch., 1–118 (2016)
9. DIF: Decentralized identity foundation. https://identity.foundation/
10. Ethereum Name Services: Decentralised naming for wallets, websites, and more. https://ens.domains/
11. Fan, X., Chai, Q., Xu, L., Guo, D.: DIAM-IoT: a decentralized identity and access management framework for Internet of Things. In: Proceedings of the 2nd ACM International Symposium on Blockchain and Secure Critical Infrastructure, pp. 186–191 (2020)
12. Friese, I., Heuer, J., Kong, N.: Challenges from the identities of things: introduction of the identities of things discussion group within kantara initiative. In: 2014 IEEE World Forum on Internet of Things (WF-IoT), pp. 1–4. IEEE (2014)
13. Guarnizo, J., Szalachowski, P.: PDFS: practical data feed service for smart contracts. In: Sako, K., Schneider, S., Ryan, P.Y.A. (eds.) ESORICS 2019. LNCS, vol. 11735, pp. 767–789. Springer, Cham (2019). https://doi.org/10.1007/978-3-030-29959-0_37
14. Guo, B., Lu, Z., Tang, Q., Xu, J., Zhang, Z.: Dumbo: faster asynchronous bft protocols. In: Proceedings of the 2020 ACM SIGSAC Conference on Computer and Communications Security (CCS), pp. 803–818 (2020)
15. He, S., et al.: Blockchain-based automated and robust cyber security management. J. Parallel Distrib. Comput. (2022)
16. He, S., Lu, Y., Tang, Q., Wang, G., Wu, C.Q.: Blockchain-based p2p content delivery with monetary incentivization and fairness guarantee. IEEE Trans. Parallel Distrib. Syst. **34**(2), 746–765 (2022)
17. He, S., Tang, Q., Wu, C.Q., Shen, X.: Decentralizing IoT management systems using blockchain for censorship resistance. IEEE Trans. Ind. Inf. (TII), 715–727 (2019)

18. Kate, A., Huang, Y., Goldberg, I.: Distributed key generation in the wild. IACR Cryptol. ePrint Arch., 377 (2012)
19. Keller, M.: Mp-spdz: a versatile framework for multi-party computation. In: Proceedings of the 2020 ACM SIGSAC Conference on Computer and Communications Security (CCS), pp. 1575–1590 (2020)
20. Khan, M.A., Salah, K.: IoT security: review, blockchain solutions, and open challenges. Futur. Gener. Comput. Syst. **82**, 395–411 (2018)
21. Luecking, M., Fries, C., Lamberti, R., Stork, W.: Decentralized identity and trust management framework for Internet of Things. In: IEEE International Conference on Blockchain and Cryptocurrency (ICBC), pp. 1–9. IEEE (2020)
22. Mahalle, P.N., Anggorojati, B., Prasad, N.R., Prasad, R.: Identity authentication and capability based access control (iacac) for the internet of things. J. Cyber Secur. Mobil. 309–348 (2013)
23. Maram, D., et al.: Candid: can-do decentralized identity with legacy compatibility, sybil-resistance, and accountability. In: 2021 IEEE Symposium on Security and Privacy (SP), pp. 1348–1366. IEEE (2021)
24. Microsoft: Decentralized identity. https://query.prod.cms.rt.microsoft.com/cms/api/am/binary/RE2DjfY
25. Microsoft: Identity Overlay Network (ION). https://github.com/decentralized-identity/ion
26. Ritzdorf, H., Wüst, K., Gervais, A., Felley, G., Capkun, S.: TLS-N: non-repudiation over TLS enabling ubiquitous content signing. In: Network and Distributed System Security Symposium (NDSS) (2018)
27. Samir, E., Wu, H., Azab, M., Xin, C.S., Zhang, Q.: DT-SSIM: a decentralized trustworthy self-sovereign identity management framework. IEEE Internet Things J. (2021)
28. Sharma, A., Schuhknecht, F.M., Agrawal, D., Dittrich, J.: Blurring the lines between blockchains and database systems: the case of hyperledger fabric. In: Proceedings of the 2019 International Conference on Management of Data (SIGMOD), pp. 105–122 (2019)
29. Sousa, J., Bessani, A., Vukolic, M.: A byzantine fault-tolerant ordering service for the hyperledger fabric blockchain platform. In: 2018 48th annual IEEE/IFIP International Conference on Dependable Systems and Networks (DSN), pp. 51–58. IEEE (2018)
30. Vitalik, B.: A next-generation smart contract and decentralized application platform. White paper (2014)
31. W3C: Decentralized Identifiers (DIDs) v1.0: core architecture, data model, and representations. https://www.w3.org/TR/did-core/
32. W3C: DID Methods. https://www.w3.org/TR/did-spec-registries/#did-methods
33. W3C: DID Specification Registries: the interoperability registry for decentralized identifiers. https://www.w3.org/TR/did-spec-registries/
34. W3C: Verifiable credentials data model v1.1. https://www.w3.org/TR/vc-data-model/
35. Weingaertner, T., Camenzind, O.: Identity of Things: applying concepts from self sovereign identity to IoT devices. J. Brit. Blockchain Assoc., 21244 (2021)
36. Yin, J., et al.: SmartDID: a novel privacy-preserving identity based on blockchain for IoT. IEEE Internet Things J. (2022)
37. Zhang, F., Cecchetti, E., Croman, K., Juels, A., Shi, E.: Town crier: an authenticated data feed for smart contracts. In: Proceedings of the 2016 ACM SIGSAC Conference on Computer and Communications Security (CCS), pp. 270–282 (2016)

38. Zhang, F., Maram, D., Malvai, H., Goldfeder, S., Juels, A.: Deco: liberating web data using decentralized oracles for tls. In: Proceedings of the 2020 ACM SIGSAC Conference on Computer and Communications Security (CCS), pp. 1919–1938 (2020)
39. Zhu, X., Badr, Y.: Identity management systems for the internet of things: a survey towards blockchain solutions. Sensors, 4215 (2018)
40. Zhu, X., Badr, Y., Pacheco, J., Hariri, S.: Autonomic identity framework for the internet of things. In: 2017 International Conference on Cloud and Autonomic Computing (ICCAC), pp. 69–79. IEEE (2017)

Enhancing Robustness of Smart Contracts Through Declarations

R. K. Shyamasundar[(✉)], Snehal Borse, and Mohammad Ummair

Department of Computer Science and Engineering, Indian Institute of Technology, Bombay, Mumbai 400076, India
rkss@cse.iitb.ac.in

Abstract. Run-time monitoring has been one of the widely used techniques to realize robust smart contracts. In this paper, we show how we can abstract aspects of run-time monitoring through declarations of programming languages so that a majority of run-time monitoring code required for preserving the intended semantics of Solidity and thereby overcome vulnerabilities can be instrumented automatically at compile time itself. For illustrative purposes, we use Solidity and call the augmented Solidity language Solidity^D. Solidity^D syntactically is identical to Solidity except for declarations. The declarations preserve the intended semantics of various constructs and thus overcome a large number of vulnerabilities. We illustrate how a vast variety of vulnerabilities encountered in programming smart contracts in Solidity are overcome through declarations. Declarations envisaged in Solidity^D are similar to that used in classic concurrent programming languages and are easily visualizable by the programmer. Declarations lead to automatic introduction of run-time code at compilation time needed to satisfy various executional constraints needed to satisfy the semantic requirements of declarations. Further, we demonstrate that Solidity^D, can be automatically transformed to pure Solidity: thus, enabling an effective debugging at source level rather than at the byte or EVM level. Another important outcome of using Solidity^D, is that it can be effectively used for asserting coarse-grained properties of declarations. Such a feature leads to gaining trust in the usage of smart contracts.

Keywords: Smart contract · Blockchain · EVM · Correctness · Debugging

1 Introduction

As smart Contracts handle and transfer assets of considerable value, it is crucial that their implementation be secure against attacks. There have been several attacks that have exploited existing vulnerabilities in smart contracts. Functioning and deployment of smart contracts is somewhat different from that of classical programming environments:(i) once a smart contract is up and running, changing it, is very complicated and nearly infeasible, (ii) one of the reasons is

J. Feng et al. (Eds.): ICBC 2024, LNCS 15425, pp. 50–68, 2025.
https://doi.org/10.1007/978-3-031-77095-1_4

that when a contract is created, it needs to be immutable, and (iii) once deployed on the blockchain it stays there forever. If we find a defect in a deployed smart contract, a new version of the contract has to be created and deploy a new version of an existing contract by consensus; however, data stored in the previous contract does not get transferred automatically to the newly refined contract. There is a need to manually initialize the new contract with the past data that makes it very cumbersome. Similarly, neither updating a contract nor rolling back an update is possible; this greatly increases the complexity of implementation and places a huge responsibility while being deployed initially on the blockchain.

Smart contract languages today are derived from extensions of general purpose languages like Javascript. While such a similarity make smart contract languages look familiar to software developers, it is inadequate to accommodate domain-specific requirements/constraints of digital contracts. Smart contracts have not only shed light on the benefits of digital contracts but also on their potential risks. Some of the prominent smart contract languages are Solidity [20], GO [3], etc. Like all software, smart contracts can contain bugs and its' vulnerabilities can be exploited that can have direct financial consequences. Thus, it is very important to have a sound methodology, that is practical enough for use by a large community of smart contract programmers to check contracts for crucial properties. Solidity is one of the widely used languages for programming smart contracts. It has been designed for Ethereum architecture. Several security vulnerabilities in Ethereum smart contracts have been discovered both by hands-on development experience, and by static analysis of contracts on the Ethereum Blockchain. These vulnerabilities have been exploited by several attacks on Ethereum, causing huge loss of money. Some of the major deficiencies of existing explorations are (i) analysis is based on the bytecode generated for Ethereum rather than smart contracts in Solidity, and (ii) analysis is limited and approximate and have severe limitations for usage due to over-/ or under-approximation. Here, we address the following problem:

> From the stark resemblance of Solidity programs with that of distributed programs, we arrive at a concurrent programming language approach for embedding the intended semantics of Solidity programs similar to that of classical declarations used in concurrent programming languages – thus, realizing automatic instrumentation of constraints corresponding to declarations leading to robustness and extensibility.

The main rationale for smart contracts has been to enforce contracts safely among the stakeholders. Runtime verification/monitoring has been explored for Solidity in [9,22]. The framework proposed in [22] prevents exploitation of a major class of vulnerabilities using programmers' annotations for smart contract programs. Annotations mimic declarations of concurrent programming languages so that the underlying run-time monitors can be automatically generated. The annotations simply reflect the intended semantics on the execution of programs relative to the object state relative to observables like method calls, exceptions, etc. Such a framework further adds to the advantage of debugging at the source level as the original structure is preserved and also enhances the trust of the user as the run-time monitoring annotations provide an assertion-outline of the contract.

In this paper, we show how such a run-time monitoring framework can be embedded in Solidity through declarations, referring to the enriched programming language as, Solidity^D, that is syntactically identical to Solidity except for the declaration part. We further build a program transformer to transform Solidity^D programs into pure Solidity programs. We demonstrate how a vast variety of vulnerabilities encountered in programming smart contracts in Solidity no longer remain when programmed in Solidity^D. Declarations are simple, and intuitive easily visualizable by a general programmer and are effectively used for run-time monitoring to generate executional constraints needed to satisfy semantic constraints imposed by declarations. Further, extensibility properties [25] of programming languages embedded in Solidity^D, facilitates guarded execution that can be leveraged by the programmer effectively. The transformation of Solidity^D program into Solidity has the distinct advantage of debugging at source level and it provides an effective assertion outline of the contract - thus, enhancing the trust on the smart contract.

2   Shared Variable Distributed Programming Languages

Programming languages for concurrent and distributed computing was one of key areas of research in 1980's [12]. The main rationale of specification (declaration) section of a concurrent program was meant to capture the interaction of processes [2,24] and the interaction of shared resources with processes. Andrews [2] suggests the following four important goals of concurrent programming languages: expressiveness, data integrity, security and verifiability. There have been a variety of concurrent programming languages oriented keeping all or some of these objectives. In early stages, languages were designed keeping in view the correctness – usually realized through a discipline of usage through specification formally or through declarations informally. For instance, one of the early well designed languages, Ada, was quite disciplined from a concurrent perspective; here integrity was realized through mutual exclusive access of shared resources. For this reason, Ada rendezvous was considered inefficient as it did not permit concurrency even when the operations were non-interfering. There have been lot of research to realize efficiency/performance without foregoing correctness. For instance, [24] explored a language structure to realize data integrity without unnecessary mutual exclusion. Considering many of the efforts in this area, we can say that a shared variable programming language is essentially a set of processes and resources (shared) whose broad structure (there could be multiple resources and processes) is depicted in Table I.

Keeping in view, the similarities between multi-transactional behaviours of smart contracts in Ethereum and classical problems of shared-memory concurrency (cf. [13,21]), we shall first discuss a general structure of shared variable distributed programming languages.

```
Process <process name ... >
Import ....          (* Classical syntax *)
Body
end Process   ...
MODSPEC Shared < Resource name>
IMPORT < components being imported into the  Module>
Export < components being expored outside the Module>
INVAR  < invariance on resource>
CONSTRAINTS  (*for interaction among processes and   resources Is
                              specified in varied forms  *)
TRANS   (* various oper./fun./proc. that operate On the resource *)
Entry procedure p1 (...)
Entry procedure p2 (...) ...
Entry procedure pn (...)
end ModSPEC
MODBODY ...
...
end MODBODY
```

Table I. General Structure of a Distributed Program

Clauses Import/Export highlight resources/ services that can imported or exported. The clause INVAR highlights invariant property of the underlying resources. Clauses in the section CONSTRAINTS, vary based on the permitted interaction of processes and access of shared resources. For instance, [24] requisite declarative clauses have been introduced so that data integrity can be realized without enforcing mutual exclusion unnecessarily and a methodology of establishing formal correctness through interference freedom proofs among processes and resources under the given constraints is described. The section TRANS highlights the operations that are possible on the resource. The MODBODY describes implementation of the operations. Below, we define the declarative structure of Solidity^D. Formal semantics can be derived on the lines of [24].

3   Solidity^D: Solidity with Declarations

Solidity^D has a specification part and a body part for each contract. The body part remains the same as in Solidity. A typical program structure in Solidity^D is shown in Table II.

```
begin_DECLARATIONS
IMPORT (* Interpretation is Classical*)
EXPORT(* Interpretation is Classical*)
(* Constraints on smart Contracts are captured by declarations as given below *)
NONRENTRANT (...)
PARALLEL (...)
ACCESS (...)
INVAR ...
CONSTRAINTS ... (eg., mutual exclusion of operations)
end_DECLARATIONS
```

```
BEGIN_Contract_COIN
  contract Coin {
    //The keyword "public" makes variables accessible from other contracts
    address public minter;
    mapping (address => uint) public balances;
    // Events allow clients to react to specific
    // contract changes you declare
    event Sent(address from, address to, uint amount);
    // Constructor code is only run when the contract is created
    constructor() public {
        minter = msg.sender;
    }
    // Sends an amount of newly created coins to an address only to be called
    // by the contract creator
    function mint(address receiver, uint amount) public {
        require(msg.sender == minter);
        require(amount < 1e60);
        balances[receiver] += amount;
    }
    // Sends an amount of existing coins from any caller to an address
    function send(address receiver, uint amount) public {
        require(amount <= balances[msg.sender],
                "Insufficient balance.");
        balances[msg.sender] -= amount;
        balances[receiver] += amount;
        emit Sent(msg.sender, receiver, amount);
    }
}
    END_Contract_COIN
```

Table II. Typical Structure of a Program in Solidity[D]

Interpretation of the clauses given in table II are given below:

1. IMPORT/EXPORT are the classical clauses for importing/exporting objects or services; useful for typecasting and authentication of oracles etc.
2. PARALLEL clause defines procedures that could operate in parallel; one could specify either the set of procedures that could be invoked concurrently or specify procedures that can have multiple concurrent invocations either on a single thread or multiple threads.
   (a) PARALLEL (p1, p2): denotes that p1, p2 can execute in concurrently; that means, p1 and p2 can be executing in the environment concurrently. The general syntax is (p1,p2), ... (pj,pk); all pairs of processes that can execute concurrently is to be explicitly defined. Note that this takes into account interacting contracts.
   (b) PARALLEL (p1, p1): is interpreted as p1 can be invoked concurrently by two threads.
   (c) PARALLEL (Nil): denotes that none of the procedures/functions specified in the contracts can execute in parallel.
3. NONRENTRANT p1,p2, ...pr: p1, ..., pn are non-reentrant procedures/functions on the same thread.

4. ACCESS clause defines the order of invocation of procedures/functions - specifies transactions, on each thread.
   (a) For instance, ACCESS (OPEN, WRITE, CLOSE) corresponds to saying that OPEN has to be applied first followed by write, and then followed by CLOSE by the same process (thread). In a sense, it provides a structure of transactions. This will enable to decide whether concurrent (interleaving) execution of transactions is permitted or not.
   (b) General structure is a regular expression over procedures or functions that form the transaction [6]; path expressions proposed in [9] brought out such specifications for synchronization of processes.
5. CONSTRAINTS: could be other constraints like guarded execution etc., the programmer would like to enforce while executing the operations.

3.1 An Illustration of Solidity^D Program

For want of space, we shall illustrate only the declaration part for the Original SimpleDAO shown in Fig. 2a that would make it non-reentrant. The SimpleDAO program shown in Fig. 2a with the above declarations is indeed reentrant-free is shown in Sect. 4.2.

```
contract SimpleDAO {
    mapping (address => uint256) public credit;
    constructor() payable public { donate();}
\%\%BEGIN\_SimpleDAO\_Declaration
\%PARALLEL (donate, donate);
\%NONREENTRANT withdraw;
\%\%END\_SimpleDAO\_Declarations
```

Fig. 1. Declarations for the SimpleDAO Program (Fig. 2a)

4 Vulnerabilities: Solidity vs Solidity^D

Varieties of vulnerabilities have been articulated in [4, 8, 21] like non-reentrancy, concurrent execution, type casting, exceptions etc. In this section, we shall illustrate a few of the vulnerabilities like non-reentrancy, concurrent execution traces etc., that have been exploited in Solidity. In the following, we shall illustrate the reentrancy vulnerability in Solidity and how it is overcome naturally in Solidity^D.

4.1 Illustrating Reentrant Vulnerability in Solidity

The well-known DAO attack which happened to steal a big amount of money was due to the reentrancy vulnerability [22]. Consider the simple DAO shown in Fig. 2a and the attacker code shown in Fig. 2b. Steps given below capture the scenario of the attack:

1. Publish contract Mallory with address "xyz".
2. Assume Mallory donates 100 ethers to SimpleDAO i.e., credit["xyz"]=100.
3. Let the adversary account be at address "123".
4. "123" transfers 100 ethers to "xyz". This invokes the fallback function of Mallory, which internally invokes withdraw function of DAO with amount=100.
5. msg.sender.call.value(amount)() invokes the fallback function of Mallory.
6. Credit of Mallory will never be changed and thus, all the money from DAO will be transferred to Mallory (even if Mallory invested only 100 ethers).
7. Recursion is continued till either the gas is exhausted or the balance becomes 0.

```
3 ▾ contract SimpleDAO {
4      mapping (address => uint256) public credit;
5
6 ▾    constructor() payable public {
7          donate();
8      }
9
10 ▾   function donate() payable public{
11         credit[msg.sender] += msg.value;
12     }
13
14 ▾   function withdraw(uint256 amount) public{
15 ▾       if (credit[msg.sender]>= amount) {
16             msg.sender.call.value(amount)("");
17             credit[msg.sender]-=amount;
18         }
19     }
20
21 ▾   function queryCredit(address to) public view returns (uint256) {
22         return credit[to];
23     }
24 }
```

```
26 ▾ contract Mallory2 {
27     SimpleDAO public dao;
28     address payable owner;
29
30 ▾   constructor(SimpleDAO addr) public payable{
31         owner = msg.sender;
32         dao = addr;
33     }
34
35 ▾   function attack() public payable{
36         dao.donate.value(1)();
37         dao.withdraw(1);
38     }
39
40 ▾   function getJackpot() public{
41         dao.withdraw(address(dao).balance);
42         owner.transfer(address(this).balance);
43     }
44
45 ▾   function() external payable{
46         dao.withdraw(1);
47     }
48 }
```

(a) Original SimpleDAO   (b) Attacker Contract Mallory

Fig. 2. SimpleDAO and an Attacker

The attack was possible due to the fact that **withdraw()** function was expected to be non-reentrant; the execution violated the constraint and succeeded in getting into attacker's fallback function. In fact, Solidity document [10] gives the following warning: *Any interaction with another contract imposes a potential danger, especially if the source code of the contract is not known in advance. The current contract hands over control to the called contract and that may potentially do just about anything. Even if the called contract inherits from a known parent contract, the inheriting contract is only required to have a correct interface. The implementation of the contract, however, can be completely arbitrary and thus, pose a danger. In addition, be prepared in case it calls into other contracts of your system or even back into the calling contract before the first call returns. This means that the called contract can change state variables of the calling contract via its functions. Write your functions in a way that, for example, calls to external functions happen after any changes to state variables* *in your contract so your contract is not vulnerable to a exploit.* It must be noted that the simpleDAO contract is already on the blockchain, and hence, it will have its issues to predict future user contracts like Mallory.

```
contract SimpleDAO {
    mapping (address => uint256) public credit;

    constructor() payable public {
        donate();
    }

    function donate() payable public{
        callStack.push("donate");
        credit[msg.sender] += msg.value;
        delete callStack[callStack.length-1];
        callStack.length--;
    }

    string[] callStack; //Injected code

    function withdraw(uint256 amount) public{
        checkReentrancy("withdraw"); //Injected code
        callStack.push("withdraw"); //Injected code

        if (credit[msg.sender]>= amount) {
            msg.sender.call.value(amount)("");
            credit[msg.sender]-=amount;
        }

        delete callStack[callStack.length-1]; //Injected code
        callStack.length--; //Injected code
    }

    //Injected function
    function checkReentrancy(string memory functionName) public {
        uint flag;
        if(callStack.length > 0){
            for(uint i=callStack.length; i>0; i--) {
                if(keccak256(abi.encodePacked(callStack[i-1]))==
                keccak256(abi.encodePacked(functionName))) {
                    flag = 0;
                    break;
                }
            }
        } else {
            flag = 1;
        }

        require(flag==1, "Reentrant!!");
    }

    function queryCredit(address to) public view returns (uint256) {
        return credit[to];
    }
}
```

Fig. 3. Modified SimpleDAO To overcome Re-entrancy

4.2   Reentrancy-Free Program in Solidity

The basic idea is to forbid non-reentrant functions to be invoked again while it is active. Due to boolean variables as well as termination, realizing it requires runtime checks and hence, run-time monitoring methodology would be a choice. Thus there is a need to instrument the program shown in Fig. 2a with guard conditions such that the "withdraw" function shall remain non-re-entrant. This is realized through instrumenting the program using *require()* function of Solidity. Informally, the instrumentation or transformation is achieved by maintaining an array, say callStack, to store all the functions that could be called from a contract. Using the array, we track functions that are already executing (not yet terminated) in a contract. A function call is said to be reentrant, if it already exists in the callStack (not yet-terminated) and the checking is done through the Solidity function *require()*. The reentrancy check is done before executing the body of a function. The modified functions of SimpleDAO are shown in Fig. 3. In the modified program, when withdraw is called for the 2nd time, execution is reverted[1] due to the require() statement in the *checkReentrancy()* function.

4.3   Reentrant Free DAO Program in Solidity^D

SimpleDAO program shown in Fig. 2a in Solidity can be written in Solidity^D to eliminate the reentrancy of **withdraw** by including the declarations shown in Fig. 1.

Note that between BEGIN_Proc_declaration[2] and END_Proc_declaration which themselves are starting with "%%" are the two declarations each beginning with "%" (i) PARALLEL: declares that the function **donate** can be instantiated in parallel and but none of the other functions, and (ii) NONREENTRANT: declares that the function **withdraw** needs to be monitored for reentrancy (or saying that it is not recursive).

If we ignore the declarations, the program is exactly the same as the original DAO program. Our program transformer (cf. Sect. 6) takes Solidity^D program and transforms to program in Solidity. For instance, it takes the SimpleDAO program shown in Fig. 2a and transforms it to Fig. 3 – thus introducing the run-time monitors automatically. The automatic crafting of run-time monitors derived from declarations is a distinct advantage of Solidity^D.

There is another variant of the re-entrant attack due to underflow/overflow described in [22]. Such an attack can be overcome by using the following declaration in the corresponding DAO smart contract: **IMPORT arithmetic SafeMath**.

For instance, the DAO program described in Fig. 3 in [22], with the above declaration leads to generating the following header snippet for the Solidity compiler by our translator:

```
pragma solidity ^0.8.0;
    import "https://github.com/
    Sharron4me/Solidity-SafeMath-
    Version0.6/blob/main/safemath.sol";
    (*REST OF THE PROGRAM SNIPPET ARE THE SAME AS the ORIGINAL*)
```

Our solution has its own version of SafeMath library that was created by *Open-Zeppelin* [18]. The solution encapsulates all the references to arithmetic operations present in the solidity program to ensure that no arithmetic overflow or

---

[1] As per the semantics of *require()*.
[2] The semantics of the declarations are described in Sect. 2.

underflow takes place. The program throws an exception if overflow or underflow takes place in solidity program – thus making the attack ineffective. Note that SafeMath library of Solidity handle only binary expressions; our library deals with complete expressions.

4.4 Vulnerabilities Due to Concurrent Execution

Even though EVM execution is single threaded, transactions are submitted in parallel, and miners may reorder and interleave those transactions arbitrarily [21,26]. For this reason, it is possible to have data races as well as arbitrary (nondeterministic) transaction orders.

Transaction Order Nondeterminism: Figure 4, shows a simple Solidity contract GetterSetter containing two functions. get function allows a user to query the contract for the balance and the set function allows a user to update the balance with the value passed as argument and return the old value of the balance. Concurrent execution leads to nondeterministic results is shown through two scenarios given below:

Scenario 1:

1. C1 calls set(100); C1 calls get(); - returns 100
2. C2 calls set(50); C2 calls get(); - returns 50

Scenario 2:

1. C1 calls set(100); C2 calls set(50);
2. C1 calls get(); - returns 50
3. C2 calls get(); - returns 50 Nondeterminism depicted in (Scenario 2) is essentially due to interleaving of operations of transactions.

```
3 ▾ contract GetterSetter {
4       uint private balance;
5
6 ▾     function get() public returns(uint) {
7           return balance;
8       }
9
10 ▾    function set(uint x) public returns(uint) {
11          uint t = balance;
12          balance = x;
13          return t;
14      }
15  }
```

Fig. 4. Original Getter Setter Contract

Refining Getter-Setter Program to Restrict Transaction Order. Nondeterminacy in the Getter-Setter problem arises due to either (i) processes (users) accessing the resource in different order or due to the nondeterministic execution of the underlying operations invoked by the processes. Let us impose the following restrictions on the getter-setter program: (i) Only the "get" operation can be execute *concurrently; i.e., "get" and "set" cannot be concurrent and "set" also cannot execute concurrently with another "set" operation.*, and (ii) "set" can be invoked only after invoking "get". That is, the *access order* of the operations are prescribed. Enforcing the above constraints in the original getter-setter program shown in Fig. 4, results in the program shown in Fig. 5.

```
3 ▾ contract GetterSetter {
4       uint private balance;
5       address lastGetCalled;
6       mapping (address => string) public lastCall;
7
8 ▾     function get() public returns(uint) {
9           require((lastGetCalled==address(0x0) || lastGetCalled==msg.sender),
10          "concurrent execution by another contract!");
11          lastGetCalled = msg.sender;
12          lastCall[msg.sender] = "get";
13          return balance;
14      }
15
16 ▾    function set(uint x) public returns(uint) {
17          require(lastGetCalled==msg.sender,
18          "concurrent execution by another contract!");
19          require(keccak256(abi.encodePacked(lastCall[msg.sender]))
20          ==keccak256(abi.encodePacked("get")),
21          "set() should be called after get()");
22          lastCall[msg.sender] = "set";
23          uint t = balance;
24          balance = x;
25          lastGetCalled = address(0x0);
26          return t;
27      }
28  }
```

Fig. 5. Getter Setter with Concurrency & Access Control

Getter-Setter Program in Solidity^D. Adding the following declaration snippet:
%%BEGIN_GetSet_Declarations
    PARALLEL (GET, GET)
    ACCESS (GET SET)
%%END_GetSET_Declarations
to the program shown in Fig. 4 at the beginning as shown previously, the behaviour of the original program will be restricted and will not have any nondeterminacy. I.e., akin to the case of DAO problem of Sect. 4.1, program shown in Fig. 5 will be automatically derived from the program of Fig. 4 using the declarations.

5   Programming Methodology for Solidity^D

Declaration clauses (phrases) have been coined keeping in view the patterns that have lead to exploitation of vulnerabilities in Solidity. Declarations capture succinctly the constraints needed to preserve the intended executional semantics of Solidity. For instance,

1. In the GetterSetter problem, it is the *order* in which different processes (users) access the resource or whether a concurrent access are permitted by the designer.
2. In DAO problem, the function "withdraw" is expected to be *non-reentrant*.

The crux of abstractions requires identifying required patterns of expected behaviour of operations using declaration clauses in the CONSTRAINTS section of Solidity^D. Declarations given by the programmer enables the translator to insert the necessary run-time monitoring code to realize the intended semantics; naturally this enhances the productivity of the programmer.

Further Illustrations
1. Limited resources like tokens, assets, or computational resources are frequently used in smart contracts. By placing restrictions on the number of operations that may be carried out within a given period of time aids in preventing excessive consumption of resources. This leads to equitable and effective resource distribution among participants. Rate limiting can help mitigate the risk of distributed denial of service (DDOS) attacks. By imposing restrictions on the number of function calls or transactions, the contract can prevent malicious actors from overwhelming the system with an excessive number of requests, thus maintaining availability and preventing disruption of the contract's functionality. This is illustrated, by an user adding limit on the rate of calling a function below:

```
pragma solidity ^0.4.17;
contract Store{
    mapping(address => uint) public balances;
    uint last_called = now;
    modifier wait(uint t) {
        if (now >= enabledAt) {
            last_called = now + t;
            -;}}
    function getBalance()
noReentrancy public wait(1 minutes){
        return address(this).balance;}
}
```

On similar lines, we can create "Balance Limit" extension.

2. Mutex: Mutexes can be created in smart contracts to ensure that critical sections of code are executed atomically; a proper usage overcomes race conditions. We realize it in Solidity^D by adding a modifier in the smart contract. This is done through the addition of locks for those shared functions in smart contracts, illustrated below:

```
pragma solidity ^0.8.0;
 contract EtherStore {
    bool locked;
    modifier noReentrancy() {
        require(!locked);
        locked = true;
        -;
        locked = false;}
    mapping(address => uint) public balances;
    function deposit()  noReentrancy public payable {
        balances[msg.sender] += msg.value;}
    function withdraw() public {
        uint bal = balances[msg.sender];
        require(bal > 0);
        (bool sent, ) = msg.sender.call{value: bal}("");
        require(sent, "Failed to send Ether");
        balances[msg.sender] = 0;}
    function getBalance()
noReentrancy public view returns (uint) {
        return address(this).balance;
    }}
```

Remarks: The above problem can also be solved using the PARALLEL clause discussed earlier. Similarly, patterns for Unchecked Send, block-timestamp or the 'gasless send' can be derived.

3. Type Cast: Solidity compiler allows type casting a type into another type but when typecasting is used aiming to bind a contract address to a variable. However, the result is not always as intended. Looking at Fig. 6a, the function *pong* in contract Bob tells us that it intends to bind the address of contract Alice to variable c and then use c to call *ping* function of Alice. But in reality, anyone with an account on the blockchain can call the "pong" of Bob by giving it an address other than that of Alice and no error or exception will be raised. Calling *pong(address of Gim)* will neither throw an exception nor the program will stop, rather it will print "Calling ping of Gim!". Now, consider a scenario, where a malicious contract written by an attacker can indeed exploit the contract Bob by executing Bob's "pong"; the effect could be completely different than that was intended by contract Bob.

This vulnerability can also be seen as an analogy to the classic phishing attack in which an attacker attempts to obtain sensitive information of a user by disguising itself as a trustworthy entity. In the case of smart contracts. an attacker can imitate a contract by using the same function signature as the contract but changing the body of the contract by having malicious code in it and then calling the original contract with the address of the malicious contract as a function parameter. This can be seen in Fig. 6a in which contract Gim is the attacker disguising itself as Contract Alice while calling function "pong" of Bob. If proper authentication in the form of address binding is not ensured,

```
3 ▾ contract Alice {                          contract Alice {
4       event printMsg(string msg);               event printMsg(string msg);
5 ▾     function ping(uint) public retur          function ping(uint) public returns (uint) {
6           emit printMsg("Calling ping              emit printMsg("Calling ping of Alice!");
7       }                                       }
8   }                                       }
9
10 ▾ contract Bob {                          contract Bob {
11 ▾     function pong(Alice c) public{          function pong(Alice c) public{
12          c.ping(42);                             require(address(c)==0xdE6A66562c299052B1cfD24ABC1DC639d429e1d6,
13      }                                           "Address not of Alice!!");
14  }                                           c.ping(42);
15                                          }
16 ▾ contract Gim {                      }
17      event printMsg(string msg);
18 ▾     function ping(uint) public retur    contract Gim {
19          emit printMsg("Calling ping          event printMsg(string msg);
20      }                                       function ping(uint) public returns (uint) {
21  }                                               emit printMsg("Calling ping of Gim!");
                                                }
                                        }
```

(a) Contract with Type Cast vulnerability   (b) Modified contract for Type Cast

Fig. 6. Type Cast

then it can lead to the execution of a piece of code which was never intended by the programmer. Thus, appropriate binding and authentication done using declarations in Solidity^D overcomes such vulnerabilities.

5.1 Embedding Extensibility in Solidity^D

Extensible programming languages have been in use from a long time [25]. Extensible means that the language is designed to make it very easy for programmers to adapt the language to suit their needs through the addition of new programming constructs. Such a feature enables to overcome a spectrum of vulnerabilities, for instance through guarded execution of sub-contracts. Various clauses can be designed to overcome vulnerabilities in this way and embedded in Solidity^D realizing robust programs.

6 Transforming Solidity^D to Solidity

From the earlier illustrations, it can be seen that runtime checks are introduced for each of the signatures of the contracts, keeping in view the declarations. This provides the idea of algorithmically transforming Solidity^D programs to Solidity in a syntax directed way. Note that the new version of Solidity uses SafeMath library [17] that takes care of arithmetic exceptions using guard functions. A broad structure of our implementation is shown in Fig. 7.

Fig. 7. Translating Solidity^D to Solidity

The transformation requires to handle the following clauses:

1. Non-rentrancy: handled through appropriate runtime checks in the program relative to the underlying functions.
2. PARALLEL Clause: This is handled by analysing the possible signatures of operations that can plausibly execute in parallel and then instrumenting the required runtime checks automatically with respect to the procedures/functions/opertaions.
3. ACCESS Clause: Pattern of access is realized through a regular expression match for the given clause corresponding to the underlying functions/operations.
4. Type Cast: Handled through the Import/Export clause.

Solidity^D uses a recursion stack to trace the recursion calls for overcoming re-entrancy. When checking the re-entrancy, we trace through the recursion stack to check if the function call is still present in the recursion stack. Solidity ($<0.8.0>$) cannot detect Arithmetic Overflow or Underflow and even the SafeMath library overcomes only for binary operators. Our implementation considers full expressions [7, 28].

6.1 Debugging and Correctness

As Solidity^D is transformed to Solidity itself, it is obviously easy to debug programs at the source level rather than EVM code; most of the other approaches use the EVM code for debugging that requires the programmer to identify translation of code fragments - that is quite a task in itself. Note that debugging in source code is quite natural. Declarations in Solidity^D depict constraints for execution of smart contracts. As the runtime checks are on the blockchain, the user can check for himself whether appropriate constraints are satisfied as per declarations.

If we look at the transformed body of Solidity^D, it consists of constructs like "require", "assert" and "revert" that provide assertions/guarantees corresponding to declarations; the patterns used for declarations shall provide a sort trust proof outline for the user. These asserts will be on the blockchain and hence, in a sense, it enhances the trust of the user

6.2 Evaluation with Other Tools

Here, we compare with some of the tool based works of [4]. For comparisons with other works including [6,14,19,27], the reader is referred to [22]. We have evaluated our tools wrt various other tools like static analysis tools, fuzzers, symbolic analysis tools, etc. Manticure [15] is a symbolic analysis tools with the problem of false negatives and challenges of path explosion, leading to incomplete coverage. Other tools like SmartCheck is primarily a limited Solidity source code analyser or Slither focuses on intermediate representation and thus, have their own limitations in covering the class of vulnerabilities that have been experienced by programmers.

We illustrate detection of errors capabilities of Solidity^D in comparison with Mythril[3]: a tool targeted to detect common vulnerabilities including integer underflow, owner-overwrite-to-Ether-withdrawal, etc., using symbolic executors (that may even be unsound often as the exploration space is limited) through bug injection in programs.

Illustration of Succinct Error Message As Compared to MyThril: We took a sample of 50 benchmark smart contracts [11] and found that our approach detects all those errors with succinct error messages apart from handling run-time errors. Be;ow, we illustrate the form of errors shown in Mythril and Solidity^D(cf. [28]) (Table 1 and 2):

Table 1. Result Generated by our Approach

File Name	Bug Line No.	Recommendation
Buggy_10.sol	Use Of send Bug in line: 4	Change the use of msg.sender.transfer

Table 2. Result Generated by Mythril

loc	length	bug type	approach
47	2	Unchecked-Send	code snippet injection

6.3   Practical Scope for the Programmer for New Abstractions

There are several programming tricks used by programmers to realize randomness or enforce time constraints, mismatch of interpretation of private/public for realizing secrecy. These errors have also been able to handle through guarded execution through user annotations.

Another major vulnerability is that of *ether lost in transfer* - loss of *ether* happens when *ether* is sent to killed contracts or unknown addresses. This happens due to the underlying semantics of Solidity. One of the well known attacks exploiting such a vulnerability is the Parity fiasco (1-Parity and 2-Parity errors) [1]. As the general problem of detecting such losses is generally undecidable, the authors [16] have built a static analysis tool called, MAIAN, that classifies vulnerabilities into greedy, prodigal, suicidal, and posthumous statically. We have used Solidity^D, annotating the *owners* in the contract, and overcome vulnerability of losing coins forever.

Strong synchronization constraints required for ERC20 [29] can be enforced in Solidity^D, using the constraints envisaged in [23]. Solidity^D can be effectively used to overcome anomalies in enforcing *conditional requirements*, such as, *B can send Y to C only if it has received X from A* using the ACCESS clause. Such

---

[3] https://mythril-classic.readthedocs.io/en/master/about.html.

classes of contracts are in general difficult to handle and often seen as anomalous behaviour of the blockchain execution. Further, using the CONSTRAINTS clause, one can realize the *casino contract* discussed in [22].

We have applied the approach to a large number of contracts that have vulnerabilities like re-entrancy, exceptions, type cast, gasless send, block.timestamp, Tx.origin, tape cast, transaction order dependency etc., and successfully executed contracts without the vulnerabilities being exploited.

7   Conclusions

In this paper, we have described the structure of Solidity^D and illustrated how it leads to a robust programming methodology for smart contracts. We have shown how varieties of vulnerabilities like reentrant, concurrency, type cast etc., are overcome naturally in Solidity^D. There have been works like [5] to overcome re-entrancy by restricting the scope and environment that limits the way the programmers think. The translated body of Solidity^D programs shown provides an idea for the syntax directed translation of Solidity^D to Solidity. Translations reflect runtime checks instrumented that enables the programmer/auditors to correlate the code with declarations. Merits of Solidity^D are (i) Solidity^D enables the programmer to write robust smart contracts using intuitive declarations without clairvoyance and provides the power extensibility to the programmer, (ii) As Solidity^D can be transformed to Solidity debugging becomes natural and easy at the source level itself, and (iii) the extensibility property of Solidity^D becomes handy and facilitates guarded execution of functions facilitating to overcome a spectrum of vulnerabilities. The approach provides a simple methodology based on shared variable programming languages built over the years. The transformer has also a symbolic tracer that enables the checking of the validity of assertions along the path. This makes it easy to trace bugs as the translated program is also in Solidity.

To sum up, Solidity^D provides a simple methodology of abstracting expected patterns of correct execution of smart contracts through declarations (that can be enhanced due to extensibility - that is certainly a welcome feature for smart contracts that are in general dynamic) and thus, programmer need not have to re-invent some of the programming tricks and thus, increases the productivity and the confidence in the use of contracts.

References

1. Akentiev, A.: Parity multisig github. https://github.com/paritytech/parity/issues/6995
2. Andrews, G.R., McGraw, J.R.: Language features for process interaction. SIGOPS Oper. Syst. Rev. **11**(2), 114–127 (1977)
3. Androulaki, E.E.: Hyperledger fabric: a distributed operating system for permissioned blockchains. In: Proceedings of 13th EuroSys Conference, pp. 30:1–30:15. ACM, New York (2018). https://doi.org/10.1145/3190508.3190538

4. Atzei, N., Bartoletti, M., Cimoli, T.: A survey of attacks on ethereum smart contracts (SoK). In: Maffei, M., Ryan, M. (eds.) POST 2017. LNCS, vol. 10204, pp. 164–186. Springer, Heidelberg (2017). https://doi.org/10.1007/978-3-662-54455-6_8

5. Bartoletti, M., Galletta, L., Murgia, M.: A minimal core calculus for solidity contracts. In: Pérez-Solà, C., Navarro-Arribas, G., Biryukov, A., Garcia-Alfaro, J. (eds.) DPM/CBT -2019. LNCS, vol. 11737, pp. 233–243. Springer, Cham (2019). https://doi.org/10.1007/978-3-030-31500-9_15

6. Bhargavan, K., et al.: Formal verification of smart contracts: short paper. In: Proceedings of 2016 ACM Workshop on Programming Languages and Analysis for Security, PLAS 2016, New York, NY, USA, pp. 91–96 (2016)

7. Borse, S.: Solidity+: specification enhanced solidity to overcome vulnerabilities. M. Tech. Dissertation, Dept. of CSE, IIT Bombay (2019)

8. Dickerson, T., Gazzillo, P., Herlihy, M., Saraph, V., Koskinen, E.: Proof-carrying smart contracts. In: Zohar, A., et al. (eds.) FC 2018. LNCS, vol. 10958, pp. 325–338. Springer, Heidelberg (2019). https://doi.org/10.1007/978-3-662-58820-8_22

9. Ellul, J., Pace, G.J.: Runtime verification of ethereum smart contracts. In: 2018 14th European Dependable Computing Conference (EDCC), pp. 158–163 (2018)

10. Ethereum: Solidity documentation (2018). http://solidity.readthedocs.io/

11. Ghaleb, A., Pattabiraman, K.: How effective are smart contract analysis tools? evaluating smart contract static analysis tools using bug injection. In: ISSTA 2020. ACM, New York (2020)

12. Hansen, P.B., Dijkstra, E.W., Hoare, C.A.R.: The Origins of Concurrent Programming: From Semaphores to Remote Procedure Calls. Springer, Heidelberg (2002). https://doi.org/10.1007/978-1-4757-3472-0

13. Kolluri, A., Nikolic, I., Sergey, I., Hobor, A., Saxena, P.: Exploiting the laws of order in smart contracts. CoRR arxiv:1810.11605 (2018)

14. Luu, L., Chu, D.H., Olickel, H., Saxena, P., Hobor, A.: Making smart contracts smarter. In: Proceedings of 2016 ACM CCS, pp. 254–269 (2016)

15. Mossberg, M., et al.: Manticore: a user-friendly symbolic execution framework for binaries and smart contracts. In: 2019 34th IEEE/ACM International Conference on Automated Software Engineering (ASE), pp. 1186–1189 (2019). https://doi.org/10.1109/ASE.2019.00133

16. Nikolić, I., Kolluri, A., Sergey, I., Saxena, P., Hobor, A.: Finding the greedy, prodigal, and suicidal contracts at scale. In: Proceedings of 34th Annual Computer Security Applications Conference, ACSAC 2018, pp. 653–663. ACM, New York (2018)

17. OpenZeppelin: announcing the openzeppelin ecosystem stack: The secure environment for builders in your ecosystem (2024). https://www.openzeppelin.com/

18. Openzeppelin contributors: Safemath.sol (2019). https://github.com/OpenZeppelin/openzeppelin-solidity/blob/master/contracts/math/SafeMath.sol. Accessed 16 June 2019

19. Permenev, A., Dimitrov, D., Tsankov, P., Drachsler-Cohen, D., Vechev, M.: Verx: safety verification of smart contracts. In: 2020 IEEE Symposium S & P, Los Almos, CA, pp. 414–430 (2020)

20. Remix: Remix - solidity ide (2018). https://remix.ethereum.org/

21. Sergey, I., Hobor, A.: A concurrent perspective on smart contracts. In: Brenner, M., et al. (eds.) FC 2017. LNCS, vol. 10323, pp. 478–493. Springer, Cham (2017). https://doi.org/10.1007/978-3-319-70278-0_30

22. Shyamasundar, R.K.: A framework of runtime monitoring for correct execution of smart contracts. In: Chen, S., Shyamasundar, R.K., Zhang, L.J. (eds.) ICBC 2022, vol. 13733, pp. 92–116. Springer, Heidelberg (2022). https://doi.org/10.1007/978-3-031-23495-8_7

23. Shyamasundar, R.K.: ERC20: correctness via linearizability and interference freedom of the underlying smart contract. In: Proceedings of SECRYPT, pp. 557–566. SCITEPRESS (2023). https://doi.org/10.5220/0012145800003555

24. Shyamsundar, R.K., Thatcher, J.W.: Language constructs for specifying concurrency in cdl. IEEE Trans. Softw. Eng. **15**(8), 977–993 (1989)

25. Solntseff, N., Yezerski, A.: A survey of extensible programming languages. Ann. Rev. Autom. Program. **7**, 267–307 (1974). https://www.sciencedirect.com/science/article/pii/0066413874900019

26. Dickerson, T., Gazzillo, P., Herlihy, M., Saraph, V., Koskinen, E.: Proof-carrying smart contracts. In: Zohar, A., Eyal, I., Teague, V., Clark, J., Bracciali, A., Pintore, F., Sala, M. (eds.) FC 2018. LNCS, vol. 10958, pp. 325–338. Springer, Heidelberg (2019). https://doi.org/10.1007/978-3-662-58820-8_22

27. Tsankov, P., Dan, A., Drachsler-Cohen, D., Gervais, A., Bünzli, F., Vechev, M.: Securify: practical security analysis of smart contracts. In: Proceedings of 2018 ACM CCS, New York, NY, USA, pp. 67–82 (2018)

28. Ummair, M.: Solidity^D: the language solidity with declaration to prevent vulnerabilities,. M. Tech Dissertation, Dept. of CSE, IIT Bombay (2023)

29. Wikipedia contributors: Erc20 token standard—Wikipedia, the free encyclopedia (2019). https://theethereum.wiki/w/index.php/ERC20_Token_Standard. Accessed 16 June 2019

Novel Perpetual Futures Market Model Based on a Family of Asymptotic Power Curves

Thuat Do[1(✉)], Tuan-Anh Pham[2], and Tuan Tran[3]

[1] Department of Mathematics, Hong Kong University of Science and Technology, Hong Kong, China
thuat86@gmail.com
[2] Derion Protocol, Hanoi, Vietnam
[3] IDG Blockchain Labs, Hanoi, Vietnam

Abstract. This paper introduces a novel model for a decentralized perpetual futures AMM protocol, utilizing a family of asymptotic power functions. It enables the construction of permission-less perpetual markets for any underlying asset, provided price feed. We provide a rigorous mathematical formalization, derivative pricing and analysis of the model. It shows that, when properly initialized, a perpetual market is everlasting under any market conditions. Furthermore, the model represents the first-ever power perpetual market to offer no liquidation for traders and no bankruptcy for liquidity providers, breaking away from conventional unique position models and order-book in legacy perpetual exchanges.

Keyword: AMM, decentralized derivatives, decentralized finance, perpetual futures, power perpetuals

1 Introduction

Uniswap, https://uniswap.org/, since launch in November 2018, has disrupted traditional spot trading models based on order-book and has laid a solid foundation for decentralized finance (DeFi) that fully leverages on-chain execution. The protocol introduced a novel pricing formula based on inverse curves ($xy = k$, k a constant) and developed a groundbreaking spot trading mechanism and automated market-making system that was previously unseen in the financial world. Uniswap's unique value proposition is its infinite liquidity, which is unattainable by traditional trading models. The inception of Uniswap can be traced back to two of Vitalik Buterin's (the creator of Ethereum) posts [1,2] on https://ethresear.ch and https://www.reddit.com in 2018, where he discussed alternative ways to run decentralized exchanges similar to prediction markets. The first (or fundamental) principles to form any market are

- having buyers and sellers to participate on trades,

J. Feng et al. (Eds.): ICBC 2024, LNCS 15425, pp. 69–83, 2025.
https://doi.org/10.1007/978-3-031-77095-1_5

– having a pricing mechanism to help buyers and sellers complete trades (this is done by conventional order-book paradigm associated with matching engines utilized on legacy exchanges).

Uniswap followed the fundamental principles but utilizing constant product for pricing mechanism, hence removing order-book model and matching engines, making the decentralized exchange (DEX) permission-less. Uniswap and its Automated Market Making (AMM) invention set a solid foundation for the growth of decentralized finance (DeFi).

Since August 2021, derivatives exchange has emerging as a vibrant area in DeFi advancement. Various products for options, futures and perpetuals are introduced (see [3] for a comprehensive landscape by 0xperp). The pioneers were dYdX protocol with the introduction of perpetuals exchange, employing the unique position and limit order book model similarly to centralized exchanges. Following, GMX, Level Finance introduced initiatives for decentralized perpetual exchanges that combine liquidity pools, unique positions, and oracle price feed. Instead of a matching engine, GMX and Level Finance uses oracle to feed the price of underlying assets for the position open and close, liquidation, and risk management. Deri protocol offers perpetual futures, everlasting options, and power perpetual based on NFT-tokenized unique positions and AMM paradigm (adapted DodoEX's AMM model). Opyn Squeeth, intuitively, introduces fully on-chain, power-perpetual synthetic tokens using on-chain asset over-collateralization, without (unique) positions and order-book model. Mycelium also utilizes power-leverage to offer perpetuals trading and AMM paradigm onchain. Premia, Dopex, Lyra, Ribbon Finance introduced crypto options to DeFi adopting legacy option pricing models (Black-Scholes, binomial pricing or Monte-Carlo simulation).

Derivatives play a crucial role in the functioning of financial markets, especially perpetual futures in the DeFi sector. The aforementioned decentralized exchanges for perpetuals and options have two major limitations.

– Liquidation congestion: Perpetual positions are unique and tokenized as a non-fungible token (NFT). This implies not only gas-consuming but also risky congestion on mass liquidation. For examples, Ethereum can process hundreds of transactions per block, Arbitrum and other layer-2 chains can do around thousands. This is far less than centralized exchanges which can liquidate up to million of positions per second.
– LP bankruptcy: Open interest of opening positions can grow infinitely, exceeding the limited collateral margin. Thus, liquidity providers (LPs) may suffer bankruptcy in volatile markets, particularly on ill-liquid markets.

We aim to solve these problems by leveraging power perpetuals concept, introduced and investigated by many DeFi researchers, e.g. Wayne Nilsen [4]. Our goal is a perpetual AMM without liquidation congestion and LP bankruptcy.

In the next sections, we prove financial meaning of power perpetuals, then formulate pay-off functions for power perpetuals based on a family of asymptotic power functions and analyze their mathematical properties. Following, Sect. 3

provides a construction of an innovative decentralized power-perpetuals market paradigm, derived from asymptotic power curves. Section 4 prices power perpetuals under Black-Scholes assumptions. Section 5 analyzes liquidity elasticity of our model, showing that LPs never get bankrupted. Section 6 applied power perpetuals to hedge impermanent loss of liquidity providers on Uniswap and alike spot AMM-DEXes.

2 Mathematical Formalization

2.1 Power Index

Given a financial derivative, i.e. an index tracking price of a targeted underlying asset (e.g. ETH), without loss of generality. A power index of ETH is denoted as ETH^k, where $k \in \mathbb{Z}$ a non-zero integer. Given a price x of ETH, when it changes $\pm\theta\%$, the power index ETH^k values $(x \pm \frac{x\theta}{100})^k$, implying a changing rate of $((1 \pm \frac{\theta}{100})^k - 1) \times 100\%$ for the ETH^k index. In the following examples, we will see that the power $k > 0$ implies a long index, while $k < 0$ implies a short index.

Examples: If ETH price increases $(+1\%)$, then ETH^4 will increases $(1+0.01)^4 - 1 = +4.06\%$, while ETH^{-4} will decrease $(1+0.01)^{-4} - 1 = -3.9\%$. If ETH price decreases (-1%), then ETH^4 will decrease $(1-0.01)^4 - 1 = -3.94\%$, while ETH^{-4} will increase $(1-0.01)^{-4} - 1 = +4.1\%$. Thus, ETH^4 is equivalent to the long-index while ETH^{-4} is for the short-index with approximately 4 times of leverage. Greater power implies higher leverage exposure.

2.2 Financial Meaning of Power Perpetuals

People are familiar with usual compounding interest, reading

$$F = P\left(1 + \frac{r}{n}\right)^{nt},$$

where, r is the interest rate, n is the number of terms the principal amount (P), is compounding in the time t, F is the (future) value at t. To compute continuous compound interest, let $n \to \infty$, and we take the limit of the above formula

$$\lim_{n \to \infty} F = \lim_{n \to \infty} P\left(1 + \frac{r}{n}\right)^{nt} = Pe^{rt},$$

where e is the exponential constant or Euler number.

Now, assuming that Alice leverages her trades with a multiplier $k > 1$. We will show that if Alice closes her positions periodically and rolls her wealth into a renewed leveraged position, then her portfolio will behave equivalently as if she buy a power perpetual contract (see Sect. 3) with power k.

Indeed, if her current wealth is Y_t and she borrows $(k-1)Y_t$ to invest into an asset at current price X_t of the underlying asset, then by the end of the trading period, her gain will be kY_tR_t, where $R_t = \frac{dX_t}{X_t}$. We arrives at the equation

$$dY_t = kY_t\frac{dX_t}{X_t} \Rightarrow \frac{dY_t}{Y_t} = k\frac{dX_t}{X_t}.$$

This implies $Y_t = Y_0X_t^k\,X_t$ of finite variation. If X_t is a Geometric Brownian Motion with volatility σ, then by using It formula [5], we see that

$$Y_t = Y_0X_t^ke^{-0.5k(k-1)\sigma^2t}.$$

Hence we can conclude that compounding leveraged trading is approximately the same as trading with power perpetuals. In the following section, we shall utilize power functions to introduce pay-off functions for perpetual future market. However, due to the constraint of limited cash-flow, our goal is that, at any price of the indexing asset, the long value and short value are positively determined and bounded, avoiding infinite growth.

2.3   Power Pay-Off Formulas

Definition 1. *Given $\alpha, \beta > 0$, and $k > 0, R > 0$, we define a pair of dual pay-off functions:*

The long pay-off value is

$$\Phi(x) = \Phi(k,x) = \begin{cases} \alpha x^k & \text{if } \alpha x^k \le \frac{R}{2} \quad i.e. \quad x \le \left(\frac{R}{2\alpha}\right)^{1/k} \\ \\ R - \frac{R^2}{4\alpha x^k} & \text{otherwise} \quad i.e. \quad x > \left(\frac{R}{2\alpha}\right)^{1/k} \end{cases} \tag{1}$$

The short pay-off value is

$$\Psi(x) = \Phi(-k,x) = \begin{cases} \beta x^{-k} & \text{if } \beta x^{-k} \le \frac{R}{2} \quad i.e. \quad x \ge \left(\frac{2\beta}{R}\right)^{1/k} \\ \\ R - \frac{R^2x^k}{4\beta} & \text{otherwise} \quad i.e. \quad x < \left(\frac{2\beta}{R}\right)^{1/k} \end{cases} \tag{2}$$

We observe that Φ and Ψ are a concatenation of a power function and its inverse version (see Fig. 1 for an illustration). On the defined domain, Φ is strictly increasing, while Ψ is strictly decreasing. Moreover, for $m_\ell = \left(\frac{R}{2\alpha}\right)^{1/k}$ and $m_s = \left(\frac{2\beta}{R}\right)^{1/k}$, we have

$$\text{for } \quad 0 < x \le m_\ell, \quad \text{then} \quad \Phi(x) = \alpha x^k \le \frac{R}{2}, \quad \lim_{x\to m_\ell^-}\Phi(x) = \lim_{x\to m_\ell^-}\alpha x^k = \frac{R}{2},$$

$$\text{for } \quad x > m_\ell, \quad \Phi(x) = R - \frac{R^2}{4\alpha x^k} \ge \frac{R}{2}, \quad \lim_{x\to m_\ell^+}\Phi(x) = \lim_{x\to m_\ell^+}\left(R - \frac{R^2}{4\alpha x^k}\right) = \frac{R}{2},$$

for $x \geq m_s$, then $\Psi(x) = \beta x^{-k} \leq \dfrac{R}{2}$, $\lim\limits_{x \to m_s^+} \Phi(x) = \lim\limits_{x \to m_s^+} \beta x^k = \dfrac{R}{2}$,

for $0 < x < m_s$, $\Psi(x) = R - \dfrac{R^2 x^k}{4\beta} \geq \dfrac{R}{2}$, $\lim\limits_{x \to m_s^-} \Psi(x) = \lim\limits_{x \to m_s^-} \left(R - \dfrac{R^2 x^k}{4\beta} \right) = \dfrac{R}{2}$.

This implies that Φ, Ψ are continuous on $(0; +\infty)$. Further, we will prove that they are differentiable on their domains, in particular, at $m_\ell = \left(\dfrac{R}{2\alpha} \right)^{1/k}$ and $m_s = \left(\dfrac{2\beta}{R} \right)^{1/k}$, respectively.

$$\lim_{x \to m_\ell^-} \frac{d\Phi}{dx} = \frac{kR}{2} \left(\frac{2\alpha}{R} \right)^{1/k}, \qquad \lim_{x \to m_\ell^+} \frac{d\Phi}{dx} = \frac{kR}{2} \left(\frac{2\alpha}{R} \right)^{1/k};$$

$$\lim_{x \to m_s^-} \frac{d\Psi}{dx} = \frac{-kR}{2} \left(\frac{R}{2\beta} \right)^{1/k}, \qquad \lim_{x \to m_s^+} \frac{d\Psi}{dx} = \frac{-kR}{2} \left(\frac{R}{2\beta} \right)^{1/k}.$$

Additionally, Φ, Ψ are bounded and asymptotic at infinity. Thus, we call Φ and Ψ *asymptotic power dual curves* or for short *asymptotic power curves* (see examples in Fig. 1).

$$\lim_{x \to +\infty} \Phi = \lim_{x \to +\infty} \left(R - \frac{R^2}{4\alpha x^k} \right) = R, \qquad \lim_{x \to +\infty} \Psi = \lim_{x \to +\infty} \beta x^{-k} = 0.$$

The intersecting point (e.g. m_ℓ, m_s) of the two branches made up of each asymptotic curve is also the inflection point of the curve, presenting the curvature change from convex to concave (see Fig. 1). The inflection points of the two curves are the same if and only if $4\alpha\beta = R^2$. Proposition 1 is clear by the previous observations.

Proposition 1. *Given $\alpha, \beta > 0$, and $k > 0, R > 0$, we have:*

- *Φ and Ψ are continuous and differentiable on the domain $(0; +\infty)$;*
- *Φ and Ψ are asymptotic at infinity and bounded within $(0; R)$.*

Theorem 1. *For $\alpha > 0, \beta > 0$, and $R > 0$, for some $x = x_0$, if it holds true*

$$\Phi(x) + \Psi(x) \leq R \tag{3}$$

then the inequality is true for all $x \in (0; \infty)$. Moreover, equality happens if and only if $4\alpha\beta = R^2$, i.e. the two asymptotic curves are symmetric via the horizontal line $y = R/2$.

Proof. According to Eq. (1) and Eq. (2), and the inequality (3) holds true for some $x = x_0 < \min\left\{ \left(\frac{R}{2\alpha}\right)^{1/k}, \left(\frac{2\beta}{R}\right)^{1/k} \right\}$. We will prove that the inequality is true for all $x \in (0; \infty)$.

For $x = x_0 < \min\left\{ \left(\frac{R}{2\alpha}\right)^{1/k}, \left(\frac{2\beta}{R}\right)^{1/k} \right\}$, because the inequality (3) holds true for some $x = x_0$,

$$\Phi(x_0) + \Psi(x_0) = \alpha x_0^k + R - \frac{R^2 x_0^k}{4\beta} = R + \left(\alpha - \frac{R^2}{4\beta}\right) x_0^k \le R,$$

implying $\quad \left(\alpha - \frac{R^2}{4\beta}\right) x_0^k \le 0 \Leftrightarrow \alpha - \frac{R^2}{4\beta} \le 0 \Leftrightarrow \beta \le \frac{R^2}{4\alpha} \Leftrightarrow \frac{2\beta}{R} \le \frac{R}{2\alpha}. \quad (4)$

This, in turn, makes the inequality (3) holds true for all $0 < x < \left(\frac{2\beta}{R}\right)^{1/k}$,

$$\Phi(x) + \Psi(x) = \alpha x^k + R - \frac{R^2 x^k}{4\beta} = R + \left(\alpha - \frac{R^2}{4\beta}\right) x^k \le R. \quad (5)$$

By (4), for $\left(\frac{2\beta}{R}\right)^{1/k} \le x \le \left(\frac{R}{2\alpha}\right)^{1/k}$, we have $\frac{2\beta}{R} \le x^k \le \frac{R}{2\alpha}$, and it holds

$$\Phi(x) + \Psi(x) = \alpha x^k + \beta x^{-k} \le \frac{R}{2} + \frac{R}{2} = R.$$

For $x > \left(\frac{R}{2\alpha}\right)^{1/k}$, by (4), it holds true $\beta - \frac{R^2}{4\alpha} \le 0$ and

$$\Phi(x) + \Psi(x) = R - \frac{R^2}{4\alpha x^k} + \beta x^{-k} = R + \left(\beta - \frac{R^2}{4\alpha}\right) x^{-k} \le R. \quad (6)$$

When $4\alpha\beta = R^2 \Leftrightarrow \alpha = \frac{R^2}{4\beta} \Leftrightarrow \frac{R}{2\alpha} = \frac{2\beta}{R}$, it is clear that equality in (5) and (6) happens. This means $\Phi(x) + \Psi(x) = R$ for all x. The proof is now complete.

We re-state Theorem 1 and have two corollaries as follows.

Theorem 2. *For $\alpha > 0, \beta > 0, R > 0$, if this inequality condition is satisfied*

$$4\alpha\beta \le R^2, \quad (7)$$

then it holds true

$$\Phi(x) + \Psi(x) \le R$$

for all $x \in (0; \infty)$. Moreover, equality happens exactly if and only if $4\alpha\beta = R^2$, i.e. the two asymptotic curves are symmetric via the horizontal line $y = R/2$, and the inflection points of the two curves coincide at $(\frac{R}{2\alpha}, \frac{R}{2})$.

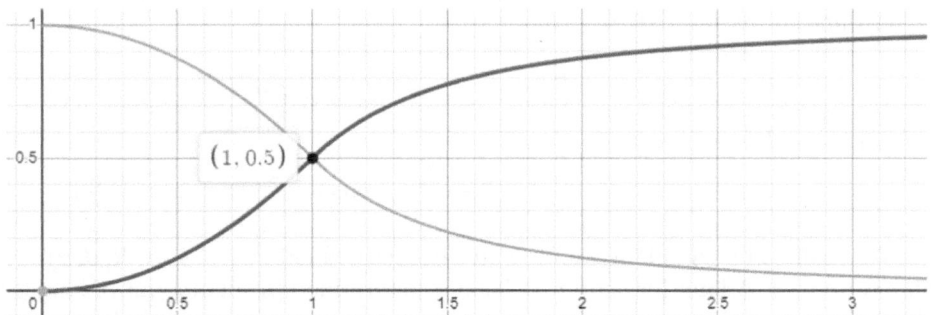

Fig. 1. An example of two (long-short) asymptotic power curves, for $R = 1, k = 2, \alpha = \beta = 0.5$. They are symmetric via the horizontal line $y = 0.5$ with the same inflection point $(1, 0.5)$.

3   A Novel Power Perpetuals Market Model

We will leverage the asymptotic power curves Φ and Ψ defined in Definition 1 as the long-short payoff functions to establish a derivatives market. Proposition 1 guarantees that long and short values are well-determined and bounded, while Theorem 1 and Theorem 2 ensure that the (long-short) market always operates normally after properly initiated despite any extremely severe cases. Formally, we define a decentralized derivatives market and payoff functions as follows.

Definition 2. *A derivatives market (or pool) is a tuple $\mathcal{M}(R, \alpha, \beta, \Phi(x), \Psi(x))$ defined by its liquidity pool (R, α, β) and the pair of long-short pay-off values $(\Phi(x), \Psi(x))$. The following conditions are to determine a valid market state, including its (first) initial state, or any state.*
   Liquidity pool (R, α, β):

- *Initiate **reserve** $R > 0$;*
- *Initiate **long coefficient** $\alpha > 0$;*
- *Initiate **short coefficient** $\beta > 0$;*
- *It must hold $4\alpha\beta \leq R^2$.*

Setting the dual pair of pay-off functions $(\Phi(x), \Psi(x))$ for power perpetuals:

- *Initiate **power leverage coefficient** $k > 0$*
- *Initiate a price oracle for indexing price $x > 0$ of the underlying asset.*
- *Initiate **long pay-off** function*

$$\Phi(x) = \Phi(k, R, \alpha, x) = \begin{cases} \alpha x^k & \text{if } x \leq \left(\frac{R}{2\alpha}\right)^{1/k} \\ \\ R - \frac{R^2}{4\alpha x^k} & \text{otherwise} \quad \text{i.e.} \quad x > \left(\frac{R}{2\alpha}\right)^{1/k} \end{cases}$$

– *Initiate* **short pay-off** *function*

$$\Psi(x) = \Phi(-k, R, \beta, x) = \begin{cases} \beta x^{-k} & \text{if } x \geq \left(\frac{2\beta}{R}\right)^{1/k} \\ \\ R - \frac{R^2 x^k}{4\beta} & \text{otherwise} \quad i.e. \quad x < \left(\frac{2\beta}{R}\right)^{1/k} \end{cases}$$

We call $\Phi(x), \Psi(x)$ a dual pair because $\Psi(x) := \Psi(k, R, \beta, x) = \Phi(-k, R, \beta, x)$. A long (or short) position is determined by an amount of long (or short) fungible tokens received from the markets. In the next, we shall compute state transitions of a pool, pricing of power perpetual positions and determine their optimal profit strategies.

3.1   Market State Transition

In this section, we shall clarify the state transition of the defined market $\mathcal{M}$ in Definition 2, which is computed whenever one of the requests (add/remove liquidity, open/close long, open/close short) is executed.

Definition 3. *At an arbitrary price x, the transition of the power perpetuals pool $\mathcal{M}(R, \alpha, \beta, \Phi(x), \Psi(x))$ to a new state $\mathcal{M}_t(R_t, \alpha_t, \beta_t, \Phi_t(x), \Psi_t(x))$ corresponding to a request execution are defined as follows (for a changing amount $0 < \Delta R, \Delta R_L, \Delta R_S$).*

$$\text{Add liquidity:}\quad R + \Delta R \rightarrow R_t, \quad \Phi(x) \rightarrow \Phi_t(x), \quad \Psi(x) \rightarrow \Psi_t(x) \tag{8}$$

$$\text{Remove liquidity:}\quad R - \Delta R \rightarrow R_t, \quad \Phi(x) \rightarrow \Phi_t(x), \quad \Psi(x) \rightarrow \Psi_t(x) \tag{9}$$

$$\text{Open long:}\quad R + \Delta R_L \rightarrow R_t, \quad \Phi(x) + \Delta R_L \rightarrow \Phi_t(x), \quad \Psi(x) \rightarrow \Psi_t(x) \tag{10}$$

$$\text{Close long:}\quad R - \Delta R_L \rightarrow R_t, \quad \Phi(x) - \Delta R_L \rightarrow \Phi_t(x), \quad \Psi(x) \rightarrow \Psi_t(x) \tag{11}$$

$$\text{Open short:}\quad R + \Delta R_S \rightarrow R_t, \quad \Phi(x) \rightarrow \Phi_t(x), \quad \Psi(x) + \Delta R_S \rightarrow \Psi_t(x) \tag{12}$$

$$\text{Close short:}\quad R - \Delta R_S \rightarrow R_t, \quad \Phi(x) \rightarrow \Phi_t(x), \quad \Psi(x) - \Delta R_S \rightarrow \Psi_t(x) \tag{13}$$

By Definition 2, we must compute other quantities in the market tuple $\mathcal{M}$, given Eqs. (8–13). We compute α_t, β_t from the previous long-short values (i.e. old states) $\Phi(x), \Psi(x)$, respectively, as follows.

- *Add liquidity* $(+\Delta R)$ and *remove liquidity* $(-\Delta R)$, from Eqs. (8, 9), We compute

$$R_t = R \pm \Delta R;$$

$$\alpha_t = \begin{cases} \dfrac{\Phi(x)}{x^k} = \alpha & \text{if } \ x \leq \left(\dfrac{R_t}{2\alpha_t}\right)^{1/k} \\[4mm] \dfrac{R_t^2}{4(R_t - \Phi(x))x^k} & \text{otherwise} \end{cases} ;$$

$$\beta_t = \begin{cases} \dfrac{\Psi(x)}{x^{-k}} = \beta & \text{if } \ x \geq \left(\dfrac{2\beta_t}{R_t}\right)^{1/k} \\[4mm] \dfrac{R_t^2 x^k}{4(R_t - \Psi(x))} & \text{otherwise} \end{cases} ;$$

Re-check $4\alpha_t\beta_t \leq R_t^2$ holding true;
Re-check $\Phi_t(R_t, \alpha_t, x) = \Phi(R, \alpha, x)$ holding true;
Re-check $\Psi_t(R_t, \beta_t, x) = \Psi(R, \beta, x)$ holding true.

- *Open long* $(+\Delta R_L)$ and *close long* $(-\Delta R_L)$, from Eqs. (10, 11), We compute

$$R_t = R \pm \Delta R_L;$$

$$\alpha_t = \begin{cases} \dfrac{\Phi(x) \pm \Delta R_L}{x^k} & \text{if } \ x \leq \left(\dfrac{R_t}{2\alpha_t}\right)^{1/k} \\[4mm] \dfrac{R_t^2}{4(R_t - (\Phi(x) \pm \Delta R_L))x^k} & \text{otherwise} \end{cases} ;$$

$$\beta_t = \begin{cases} \dfrac{\Psi(x)}{x^{-k}} = \beta & \text{if } \ x \geq \left(\dfrac{2\beta_t}{R_t}\right)^{1/k} \\[4mm] \dfrac{R_t^2 x^k}{4(R_t - \Psi(x))} & \text{otherwise} \end{cases} ;$$

Re-check $4\alpha_t\beta_t \leq R_t^2$ holding true;
Re-check $\Phi_t(R_t, \alpha_t, x) = \Phi(R, \alpha, x) \pm \Delta R_L$ holding true;
Re-check $\Psi_t(R_t, \beta_t, x) = \Psi(R, \beta, x)$ holding true.

- *Open short* $(+\Delta R_S)$ and *close short* $(-\Delta R_S)$, from Eqs. (12, 13), we compute

$$R_t = R \pm \Delta R_S;$$

$$\alpha_t = \begin{cases} \dfrac{\Phi(x)}{x^k} = \alpha & \text{if } \ x \leq \left(\dfrac{R_t}{2\alpha_t}\right)^{1/k} \\[4mm] \dfrac{R_t^2}{4(R_t - \Phi(x))x^k} & \text{otherwise} \end{cases} ;$$

$$\beta_t = \begin{cases} \dfrac{\Psi(x) \pm \Delta R_S}{x^{-k}} & \text{if } \ x \geq \left(\dfrac{2\beta_t}{R_t}\right)^{1/k} \\[4mm] \dfrac{R_t^2 x^k}{4(R_t - (\Psi(x) \pm \Delta R_S))} & \text{otherwise} \end{cases} ;$$

Re-check $4\alpha_t\beta_t \leq R_t^2$ holding true;
Re-check $\Phi_t(R_t, \alpha_t, x) = \Phi(R, \alpha, x)$ holding true;
Re-check $\Psi_t(R_t, \beta_t, x) = \Psi(R, \beta, x) \pm \Delta R_S$ holding true.

3.2   Remark

According to Condition (7) in Theorem 2, in order for the new market state $\mathcal{M}_t$ to be valid, we must check $4\alpha_t\beta_t \leq R_t^2$ holds true for all transition cases. Then, we obtain a new dual pair of asymptotic curves (corresponding with R_t, α_t, β_t) to compute the next long-short values in the following market state transition. The new long-short curves are

$$\Phi_t(x) = \Phi_t(R_t, \alpha_t, x); \quad \Psi_t(x) = \Psi_t(R_t, \beta_t, x).$$

We completely introduce a novel model for power perpetuals market based on asymptotic power curves. In next sections, we will analyze characteristics of the model in terms of derivatives pricing, leverage, decay factor. Note that, by mathematical nature, liquidation, so congestion, does not appear in our asymptotic power curve model. Moreover, liquidity providers never suffer bankruptcy, ensured by Theorem 2.

4   Pricing Power Perpetuals Without Decay Factor

Pricing a derivatives is essential in finance. In this section, under Black-Schole assumption, we will apply perpetual American option pricing model [6] to compute pricing of our power perpetuals without decay factor. Assume that the price of the power-perpetuals token defined in Definition 1 follows a geometric Brownian motion.

$$\frac{dY_t}{Y_t} = \mu dt + \sigma dW_t.$$

The equation means that the growth rate of the token price is constant μ, perturbed by an aggregate Gaussian noise of size σ-also called return volatility.

In what follows, we assume that there is no incoming traders to the pool. The fair price of any pay-off stream $f(t, X_t)$, exercised by the buyer, at an optimal stopping time τ, is given by the net present value of the pay-off under the risk-neutral probability

$$V = \max_{\tau} \mathbf{E}^*[e^{-r\tau} f(\tau, X_\tau)].$$

What is risk-neutral probability? It is an adjustment of the statistical probability under which the dynamics of token price is

$$\frac{dX_t}{X_t} = rdt + \sigma dW_t.$$

Why μ is replaced by r? Because r is the funding rate and the whole pricing methodology depends only on the hedging arguments, which relates constantly buying and selling tokens (thus the growth rate term will be removed, while cash is borrowed and lent at interest rate r).

Without loss of generality, assume that $X_0 = 1$.

4.1   Pricing Long Positions

Let's denote $a = \left[\frac{R}{2\alpha}\right]^{1/k}, C_k = \left[\frac{k+1}{2}\right]^{1/k}, L^* = aC_k$. The optimal stopping time is defined by the first passage time of the token price cross a threshold $L > 1$ that we have to determine: $\tau = \inf\{t > 0 : X_t \geq L\}$. It is straightforward to prove that

$$\mathbf{E}^*[e^{-r\tau}] = \frac{X_0}{L} = \frac{1}{L}.$$

Recall that if $a > 1$, the initial state $(X_0, Q(X_0))$, where $Q(x) = \Phi(x)/a$ belongs to the convex branch on the left, otherwise it belongs to the concave branch on the right. We consider two cases.

Case 1: $L^* > 1$. This case includes the case where the initial states belongs to the left branch $(a > 1)$ and a part of the right branch. We can prove that the optimal threshold is given by L^*. And the optimal pay-off value is

$$Q^* = Q(L^*) = 2a^k - a^{2k}[L^*]^{-k} = \frac{2k}{k+1}a^k.$$

The price of the contract is

$$V^* = \mathbf{E}^*[e^{-r\tau^*}Q^*] = \frac{Q^*}{L^*} = \frac{4k}{(k+1)^2}(L^*)^k > 1.$$

The optimal strategy is to wait until the state is a bit beyond the inflection point to the right. For example, if $k = 2, L^* = 1.1$ (i.e. traders have to wait until the price increases by 10% to exercise), then the price is 1.0755. This means that the funding rate is about 7.55%.

Case 2: $L^* < 1$ (the tail of the concave branch). We can prove that it is optimal to execute the position right at the initial time $t = 0$. This means that no trader is interested in open long position at the right tail of the pay-off curve.

4.2   Pricing Short Positions

Let's denote $b = \left[\frac{2\beta}{R}\right]^{1/k}, c = \frac{2r}{\sigma^2} < 1, C_{-k} = \left[\frac{2c}{c+k}\right]^{1/k}, L_* = bC_{-k}$. The stopping time $\tau = \inf\{t > 0 : X_t \leq L\}$. It is straightforward to prove that

$$\mathbf{E}^*[e^{-r\tau}] = \left[\frac{X_0}{L}\right]^{-c} = L^c < 1.$$

Recall that if $b < 1$, the initial state $(X_0, Q(X_0))$, where $Q(x) = \Psi(x)/\beta$ belongs to the convex branch on the right, otherwise it belongs to the concave branch on the left. We consider two cases.

Case 1: $L_* < 1$. This case includes the case where the initial states belongs to the right branch $(b < 1)$ and a part of the left branch. We can prove that the optimal threshold is given by L_*. And the optimal pay-off value is

$$Q^* = Q(L_*) = \frac{2}{b^k} - \frac{1}{b^{2k}}[L_*]^k = \frac{2k}{k+c}b^{-k}.$$

The price of the contract is

$$V^* = \mathbf{E}^*[e^{-r\tau^*}Q^*] = Q^*L_*^c = \frac{2k}{(k+c)C_{-k}}(L_*)^{-\frac{k}{c}} > 1.$$

The optimal strategy is to wait until the state is a bit beyond the inflection point to the left.

Case 2: $L_* > 1$ (the head of the concave branch). We can prove that it is optimal to execute the position right at the initial time $t = 0$. This means that no trader is interested in open short position at the left head of the pay-off curve.

5   Model Analysis

5.1   Liquidity Reserve vs Counterparty Liquidity

Counterparty in traditional finance means the other party that participates in a financial transaction. In a narrow sense, counterparties are market makers who provide liquidity and facilitate trades. In DeFi, in particular, regarding our power perpetuals markets, counterparties are liquidity providers (LPs), who provide liquidity for long and short traders. Thus, LPs are less exposed to price volatility but to impermanent liquidity loss and gain (see Sect. 5.2). Briefly, **counterparty liquidity** is provided by LPs.

Note that all **liquidity reserve** (for short, reserve) of the market is R, including counterparty liquidity and marginal funds deposited by long-short traders. By Theorem 2, total unresolved profit & loss (PnL) is $\Phi(x) + \Psi(x) \leq R$ for all x. Formally, the non-negative quantity $\mathcal{L}(x) = R - \Phi(x) - \Psi(x)$ is called **counterparty liquidity** of the market, provided and maintained by liquidity providers. Greater counterparty liquidity $\mathcal{L}(x)$ means greater liquidity reserve R, and greater liquidity reserve allows a wider price range with full leverage for traders, and vice versa. According to Equations (8, 9), (counterparty) liquidity is added or removed from the market $\mathcal{M}$ without affecting long-short values. In fact, our market model can operate normally without counterparty liquidity, i.e. only long and short traders appear in the market. However, liquidity providers should be incentivized (e.g. by decay factor) to provide more counterparty liquidity $\mathcal{L}$, hence increasing efficiency and leverage zoom for long-short traders.

By Definition 1, it is clear that optimal leverage almost lies on the left side of the inflection points, i.e. power branches of the asymptotic power curves. However, the two inflection points of the two dual long-short curves may not be the same. We will find the maximum value of counterparty liquidity for each market. Recall that the long curve Φ is strictly increasing from 0 to R, while the short curve Ψ is strictly decreasing from R to 0. Thus, they must intersect exactly at a unique point. By Theorem 2, if $4\alpha\beta = R^2$, then $\mathcal{L} = R - \Phi(x) - \Psi(x) = 0$ for all x. However, in practice, we expect a positive counterparty liquidity $\mathcal{L}$. Therefore, by Theorem 2, we only consider $4\alpha\beta < R^2 \Leftrightarrow \frac{2\beta}{R} < \frac{R}{2\alpha}$ then $\mathcal{L}(x) =$

$R - \Phi(x) - \Psi(x) > 0$ for all x. For $\left(\frac{2\beta}{R}\right)^{1/k} \leq x \leq \left(\frac{R}{2\alpha}\right)^{1/k}$, we have

$$\Phi(x) = \Psi(x) \Leftrightarrow \alpha x^k = \beta x^{-k} \Leftrightarrow x = \left(\frac{\beta}{\alpha}\right)^{\frac{1}{2k}} \quad \text{(satisfied)}.$$

We will show that the unique intersecting point $x = \left(\frac{\beta}{\alpha}\right)^{\frac{1}{2k}}$ of the two long-short curves is also the maximum point of liquidity, given $4\alpha\beta < R^2$.

$$\mathcal{L}(x) = \begin{cases} (\frac{R^2}{4\beta} - \alpha)x^k & \text{if } x < \left(\frac{2\beta}{R}\right)^{1/k} \\[2ex] R - \alpha x^k - \beta x^{-k} & \text{if } \left(\frac{2\beta}{R}\right)^{1/k} \leq x \leq \left(\frac{R}{2\alpha}\right)^{1/k} \qquad (14) \\[2ex] (\frac{R^2}{4\alpha} - \beta)x^{-k} & \text{otherwise} \end{cases}$$

Because function $\mathcal{L}(x)$ is increasing at the first interval and decreasing at the third one. At least one critical point of $L(x)$ must belong to the second (between) interval. We have

$$\mathcal{L}'(x) = -k\alpha x^{k-1} + k\beta x^{-k-1} \qquad \mathcal{L}'(x) = 0 \Leftrightarrow x = \left(\frac{\beta}{\alpha}\right)^{\frac{1}{2k}}$$

$$\mathcal{L}'(x) > 0 \Leftrightarrow x < \left(\frac{\beta}{\alpha}\right)^{\frac{1}{2k}} \qquad \mathcal{L}'(x) < 0 \Leftrightarrow x > \left(\frac{\beta}{\alpha}\right)^{\frac{1}{2k}}.$$

Thus, $x = \left(\frac{\beta}{\alpha}\right)^{\frac{1}{2k}}$ is the maximum point of $\mathcal{L}(x)$. Additionally, the function is asymptotic at infinity $\lim_{x \to +\infty} \mathcal{L}(x) = 0$ (see Fig. 2 for an illustration).

5.2   Liquidity Elasticity: Impermanent Loss & Gain

According to the previous mathematical analysis, counterparty liquidity $\mathcal{L}(x)$ (sometimes, for short, liquidity) is a smooth curve with a unique maximum and asymptotic behavior (see Fig. 2). More concretely, for a current market state, we calculate (counterpart) **liquidity elasticity** (LE) or liquidity PnL between two prices moving from x to x_t, as follows.

$$LE = \mathcal{L}(x_t) - \mathcal{L}(x) = (\Phi(x) - \Phi(x_t)) + (\Psi(x) - \Psi(x_t)).$$

If $LE > 0$, liquidity value increases; otherwise, liquidity value decreases. Observing that on the left side of the maximum point, $LE > 0$, and on the right side of the maximum point, $LE < 0$ (see Fig. 2 also).

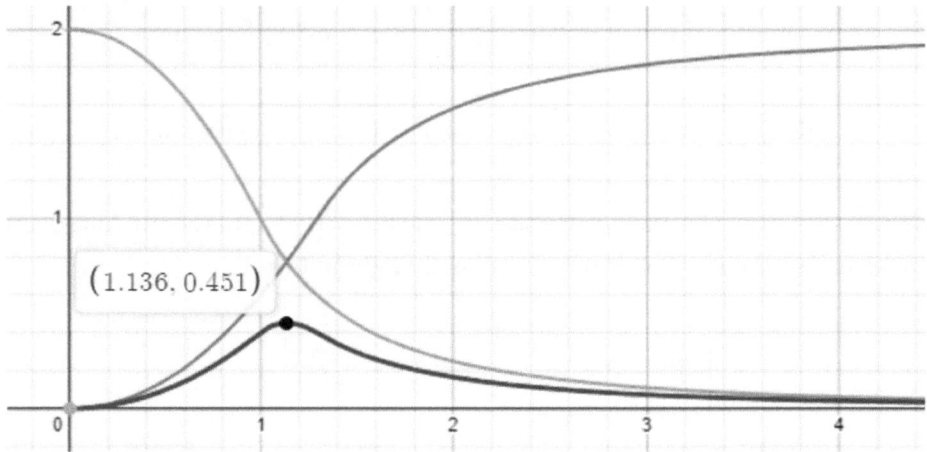

Fig. 2. Liquidity Elasticity phenomenon: long curve (red), short curve (green), counterparty liquidity curve (violet) with maximal point, for $k = 2, R = 2, \alpha = 0.6, \beta = 0.1$. (Color figure online)

Impermanent loss (IL) of LPs is a popular phenomenon of Uniswap's AMM and the likes. IL will become *permanent losses* if the price never returns to the entry price. Our market model based on asymptotic power curves has the impermanent loss phenomenon, but also impermanent gain. Formally, according to the indexing price change, we say:

– The **Impermanent loss** appears whenever liquidity elasticity $LE < 0$.
– The **Impermanent gain** appears whenever liquidity elasticity $LE > 0$.

6   Application on Perpetuals and Hedging Impermanent Loss

Power perpetuals and their applications are attracting interests from both venture capitals (Paradigm) and DeFi projects (Deri Protocol, Predy, Opyn Squeeth). Beside creating and trading power perpetuals in general, a special and meaningful use case of power perpetuals is to hedge IL on Uniswap as presented in the following (readers are referred to Lioba Heimbach et al. [7] for detailed analysis of IL on Uniswap).

Denoting S the price of ETH, x, y the quantities of ETH and USDT, respectively, then the value of liquidity position, the Delta and Gamma of the LP portfolio on Uniswap v2 are:

– $V_{v2} = xS + y = 2\sqrt{SK}$, ($K > 0$ is a given constant),
– Delta $\Delta = \frac{\partial V_{v2}}{\partial S} = \sqrt{\frac{K}{S}}$,
– Gamma $\Gamma = \frac{\partial \Delta}{\partial S} = -\frac{\sqrt{K}}{2S^{3/2}} = -\frac{\sqrt{K}}{2}S^{-3/2}$.

Given a liquidity bin $[S_l, S_u]$, the value of liquidity position, the Delta and Gamma of the LP portfolio on Uniswap v3 are:

- $V_{v3} = xS + y = L\left(2\sqrt{S} - \frac{S}{\sqrt{S_u}} - \sqrt{S_l}\right)$, ($L > 0$ is a given constant),
- Delta $\Delta = \frac{\partial V_{v3}}{\partial S} = L(\frac{1}{\sqrt{S}} - \frac{1}{\sqrt{S_u}})$,
- Gamma $\Gamma = \frac{\partial \Delta}{\partial S} = -\frac{L}{2S^{3/2}} = -\frac{L}{2}S^{-3/2}$.

We see that the greeks of LP portfolio on Uniswap v2 & v3 contain square-root and power terms, especially the Gamma part complicates the impermanent loss. Thus, hedging IL by traditional linear futures, liquidity providers must rebalance the hedging position frequently to adapt to the rapidly changing Delta. Such a process is called dynamic Delta hedging (DDH), causing a substantial cost and effort. However, it is instantly easy to hedge with power perpetual contracts. Readers are referred to [8], publish0x, and Deri Protocol for details. In general, we apply this research to implement an AMM protocol [9] for trading power perpetuals on blockchains.

References

1. Buterin, V.: Let's run on-chain decentralized exchanges the way we run prediction markets. https://www.reddit.com/r/ethereum/comments/55m04x/lets_run_onchain_decentralized_exchanges_the_way/
2. Buterin, V.: Improving front running resistance of x*y=k market makers. https://ethresear.ch/t/improving-front-running-resistance-of-x-y-k-market-makers/1281
3. 0xperp, DeFi Derivative Landscape. https://github.com/0xperp/defi-derivatives
4. Nilsen, W.: Power Claims for fun and profit (2021). https://github.com/waynenilsen/zendax/blob/master/latex/PowerClaims.pdf
5. Itô, K.: Stochastic Integral. Proc. Imperial Acad. Tokyo **20**, 519–524 (1944)
6. Privault, N.: Stochastic Finance: An Introduction with Market Examples, 1st edn. Chapman and Hall/CRC Financial Mathematics Series (2014)
7. Heimbach, Lioba, S., Eric, W.R.: Risks and returns of uniswap V3 liquidity providers. In: Proceedings the 4th ACM Conference on Advances in Financial Technologies (AFT 2022), pp. 89–101. Association for Computing Machinery, New York (2023). https://doi.org/10.1145/3558535.3559772
8. Schaller, A.J.: Hedging the Risks of Liquidity Providers, Bachelor thesis, ETH Zurich (2022). https://pub.tik.ee.ethz.ch/students/2022-FS/BA-2022-19.pdf
9. Pham, T.-A.: Derion Labs Derion protocol. https://github.com/derion-io

Improving Raft Consensus Algorithm with Relay and Lease Mechanism

Yufang Sun[1], Bing Guo[2], Daiwei Jia[3], and Songlin He[3,4(✉)]

[1] Chengdu Technological University, Chengdu 611730, Sichuan, China
syfang2@cdtu.edu.cn
[2] Sichuan University, Chengdu 610065, Sichuan, China
guobing@scu.edu.cn
[3] Southwest Jiaotong University, Chengdu 610031, Sichuan, China
[4] Manufacturing Industry Chain Collaboration and Information Support Technology Key Laboratory of Sichuan Province, SWJTU, Chengdu 610031, Sichuan, China
sohe@swjtu.edu.cn

Abstract. Consensus algorithms are critical in distributed systems, especially with the wide adoption of blockchain technology in various scenarios. For the sake of efficiency, consortium blockchains such as Hyperledger Fabric usually adopt crash fault tolerant (CFT) algorithms, i.e., Raft, to reach consensus amongst peers as entities are often authenticated and mutually trustful in a permissioned setting. Raft algorithm replicates the state among peers and therefore plays a fundamental role in ensuring strict consistency. However, with the ever-growing system scale, the leader becomes a bottleneck in Raft, considerably impacting its efficiency and scalability. In this study, we propose a consensus algorithm Praft where a relay node-based method and a lease mechanism are designed to mitigate the aforementioned issues. The details of the consensus algorithm are elaborated with its security sketch. Extensive experiments are also conducted to demonstrate its efficiency. Compared with the related solutions, e.g., etcd-raft, in the same cluster scale, Praft can decrease message load by 20%–90% and improve consensus throughput by 35%–400%.

Keywords: Consensus · Raft · Blockchain · Crash Fault Tolerance

1 Introduction

Consensus algorithms play a essential role in distributed systems. In recent years, the emergence and wide application of distributed ledger technology (DLT), or blockchain to diversified scenarios [3, 7, 11] make the consensus algorithm a hot topic in both industry and academia. Typically, consensus algorithms can be categorized from different perspectives. For instance, from the adversary model viewpoint, consensus can be either byzantine fault tolerant (BFT) where adversary can perform any misbehaviour, or crash fault tolerant where servers may be power-off and cannot provide normal service. From the communication model viewpoint, consensus algorithms can be synchronous, partial synchronous or asynchronous [2,6,15,20]. In many fields, entities are required to be authenticated, resulting in a permissioned network where entities know each other and to some degree mutually trustful. In such a setting, efficiency is of priority and therefore CFT consensus is the primary choice. We focus on the popular CFT protocol, i.e., Raft [17], in this study. It is also a key module in widely used consortium blockchain platforms such as Hyperledger Fabric.

Specifically, Raft is a consensus algorithm developed by Diego Ongaro and John Ousterhout at Stanford University [17]. It aim to make it easier understand than previous algorithms like Paxos [14] while providing strong fault tolerance and leader election capabilities. As shown in Fig. 1, Raft contains two phases of *log sync-up* and *commit*. In the log sync-up phase, clients send requests of operations to the leader (message can be forwarded to the leader), who appends the operations as log entries and broadcasts log entries to followers. The followers validate and append to their local logs. In the commit phase, when most of the nodes successfully append the logs, the leader would mark the corresponding log entries as committed in its local state machine, and then respond to the clients, and send the log entries' indexes to followers, who upon receiving the message would apply the operations to their local state machines.

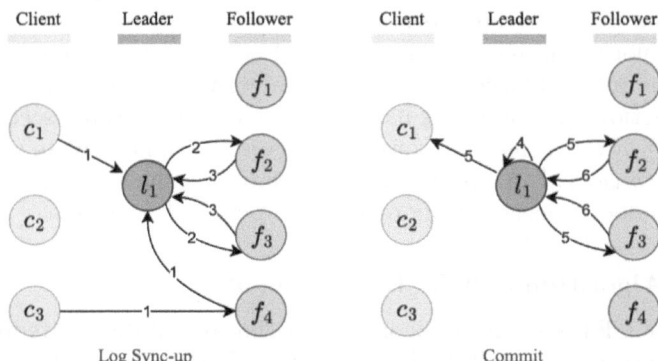

Fig. 1. The consensus process of Raft algorithm.

An observation of the Raft consensus process is that the leader takes much more message load. Consider the system contains n nodes and no log conflict occurs, the leader needs to transfer $2n + n/2 + 1$ messages while a follower only needs to handle one or two messages, leading to severe imbalance of message loads. The bottleneck of the leader node greatly hinders the efficiency and scalability of the sustainable running of the system.

Contributions. To mitigate the bottleneck brought by the leader node in Raft, we propose an improved consensus algorithm based on Raft, and our contributions can be summarized as follows.

– We propose a relay mechanism in Raft where peers in the distributed network are grouped and each group selects a relay node to delegate the consensus

message and interact with followers and leader, thus significantly mitigating the workload of the leader and improving system efficiency and scalability.
- We propose a lease mechanism in Raft to further mitigate the workload when the leader node interacts with client, thus further improving the efficiency and scalability.
- The algorithm is implemented and evaluated in a real network environment. Extensive experiments and analysis demonstrate that the proposed algorithm can ensure the required security properties with improved efficiency.

2 Background and Related Works

2.1 Blockchain and Consensus Algorithms

Blockchain can be defined as an immutable ledger for recording transactions among mutually untrusting peers in a distributed network. Nowadays the applications of blockchain have been extended to many domains [8,9,11,21] far beyond cryptocurrencies [16,19]. Blockchain usually can be categorized into three types: *public* or *permissionless*: anyone can participate or leave; (*permissioned*) *consortium*: participants are identified and known to each other, and the servers forming the blockchain network are from different organizations; (*permissioned*) *private*: similar to consortium network while the key difference is that the servers forming the blockchain network are provided or controlled by one organization. As the key module in blockchain, consensus algorithms help peers reach consensus of transactions. A consensus usually needs to satisfy three security properties [1,10]: (i) *termination*. The consensus algorithm can complete after a period of time; (ii) *agreement*. All peers would agree on a same value; (iii) *safety*. The agreed value among peers is from one honest peer in the system.

2.2 Raft Algorithm and Its Improvement

As a popular CFT consensus algorithm in the distributed systems, there are a set of literature around Raft. In particular, Huang et al. [12] paid attention to the network stability in Raft and proposed an analytical model to analyze the distributed network split probability. Fu et al. [5] proposed to improve the efficiency of Raft in Hyperledger Fabric via apportionment idea, which aims to reduce the communication complexity of leader node by involving peer node in distributing log information. Also, the leader selection strategy is designed to reduce the election time. Kim et al. [13] suggested to utilize federated learning to evaluate the criteria for selecting a more stable leader in the next round. The works in [18,22] target on improving Raft with byzantine fault tolerance, thus enhance its security while enjoying the efficiency.

3 Designs

In this section, we present the details of Praft, including the consensus process, log conflict handling and client interaction. Security analysis is conducted to show that Praft can ensure needed properties.

3.1 Consensus Process

The Praft consensus algorithm, unlike raft algorithm consisting of two phases, contains three phases, i.e., *log pre-sync, sync-up* and *commit,* as depicted in Fig. 2.

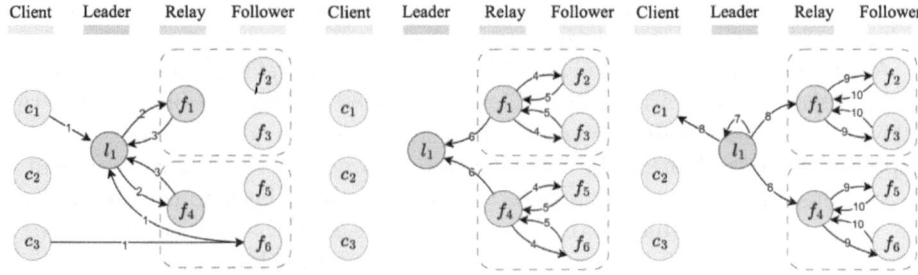

Fig. 2. The consensus process of Praft.

– **Phase I for Log Pre-Sync.** The leader node receives requests from clients, appends to local log as log entries. Then the leader selects a node from each group of followers as a relay node, and send log sync-up request to relay nodes. In this phase, each relay node acts as a follower to handle the log sync-up request from the leader, and then enters the next phase once its local log is consistent with the leader node's.
– **Phase II for Log Sync.** Each relay node, acting as a leader node in each group, sends the log sync request to all followers in its group. Then the relay node waits for followers' responses and aggregates to one message and sends the message to the leader node. Then entering the next phase.
– **Phase III for Commit.** The leader node collects all the responded message from relay nodes, and check all the responses of the syncing progress. If the log entries are synced to over half of the nodes, then the leader node would mark the corresponding log entries as committed, and reply to the clients. The the leader node sends the commit confirmation message containing log entry indexes to the relay nodes, who would forward to its group, in which followers would execute the operations in the marked log entries.

3.2 Log Conflict Handling Mechanism

The log sync efficiency between the leader node and relay nodes greatly impacts the performance of the whole consensus process. If there exist a lot of differences, the caused extra communication load may let the relay nodes not be able to sync log entries to its followers in time. In raft algorithm, if the leader node receives reject sync-up message from the followers, it would decrease the locally stored *nextIndex* value for that follower node and resend the sync request. Also, in raft there is no much impact even if there exist a lot of differences between followers and the leader since it is sufficient for the leader node to receive only half of the followers' responses. However, in Praft, the huge differences between followers and the leader would block the sync process. Hence, we introduce the log conflict handling process. The core idea lies in adding the fields *hintIndex* and *hintTerm* in the reject sync-up message such that the leader can obtain the information and know which log entry should be sent in the next sync request, and circumventing the conflicting log entries.

After completing the log sync with the leader, the relay node can be reckon as the "leader" node of its group. The relay nodes are responsible for collecting followers' responses and forward to the leader, which needs to check if all the responses are over half in the whole system. To ensure that more than half of the responses are sent to the leader, we use t_i as the collecting threshold of the i-*th* group, s_i as the amount of ignorable responses of the i-*th* group, and n_i is the number of followers in the i-*th* group. Their relationship can be expressed as $t_i = n_i - s_i$. The minimum threshold of collected responses in each group should be as $\sum_{i=1}^{p} t_i \geq \lfloor (\sum_{i=1}^{p} n_i + p + 1)/2 \rfloor - p - 1$, where p represents the number of groups in the system.

3.3   Client Interaction

For the leader node, receiving or sending huge amount of requests from or to clients may still cause performance bottleneck. For writing requests, it requires reaching consensus among all nodes via the leader node since involving updating state machine. While for reading requests, Praft always ensures the leader node to keep the latest state, which can directly return results upon reading requests. However, some situations such as node crash or network partition may trigger the leader change process, and the reading result may be from old leader nodes, leading to inconsistency. In Praft, we propose a lease mechanism to manage the leader's identity. A "isQuorum" field is employed to indicate whether the leader node is effective or not. If effective, there is no need to check heartbeat and directly respond to the client. The lease time can be defined as $leaseTime = startTime + electionTimeout \times clockDriftRate$ where *startTime* means the time point when the leader node starts log sync-up request or heartbeat, *clockDriftRate* indicates the drifted time due to process scheduling, garbage collection, or CPU clock frequency discrepancy, and typically ranges from 0 to 1. As shown in Fig. 3, after completing the log sync for most parties or receiving more than half of the followers' heartbeat responses, the leader would reset the *leaseTime* to extend the lease.

3.4   Security Sketch

Theorem 1. *The proposed* Praft *consensus algorithm satisfies security properties of safety and liveness.*

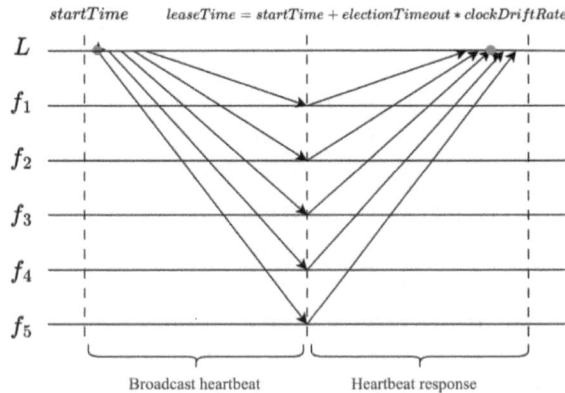

Fig. 3. The heartbeat lease mechanism in Praft.

Proof. The property safety means that the nodes in the cluster can reach consensus no matter what occurs, while liveness indicates that the nodes in the cluster can reach consensus according to clients' requests within a period of time, and non-operational case would not occur. The proposed Praft algorithm updates the communication mechanism in the log sync-up phase, introduces conflict handling strategy, and designs the reading requests handling method. Such designs would not impact the liveness and safety for the leader election and log commit phases. If followers or a relay node crashes, Praft follows the similar strategy with the raft algorithm, i.e., resending unsuccessfully handled requests to ensure crashed nodes to obtain requests after resuming. Indeed, due to the layered log sync-up mechanism of Praft, waiting for some nodes' responses may block the consensus process of the whole cluster. In this case, Praft utilizes the timeout mechanism and selects new leader node, thus assuring the consensus process can smoothly proceed. Overall, the safety and liveness properties of Praft can be guaranteed.

4   Experiment and Analysis

In this section, we analyze and present the experiment results of the implemented Praft consensus algorithm.

Experiment Setting. The hardware for conducting our experiments is desktop, which is equipped with the CPU of AMD Ryzen7 4800H (8 Cores, 16 Threads, 2.90 GHz), 16 GB DDR4 memory and 512 GB SSD. The programming language is Golang 1.20.5, the IDE is VScode and the OS is Ubuntu 18.04. We evaluate the algorithm following standard indicators, i.e., *throughput* and *latency*. To showcase its efficiency, we compare the evaluation results with the widely used *Etcd-raft* [4] consensus algorithm.

The Analysis of Average Message Load. Table 1 lists the message load of followers and leader for reaching consensus upon client's requests in different

Table 1. The comparison of average message load for leader and followers under different cluster scale.

n	r	AML_L	AML_F	AML_L/AML_F
5	1	4	3.50	1.14
5	2	6	3.00	2.00
5 (Raft)	**4**	**10**	**2.00**	**5.00**
15	1	4	3.86	1.03
15	2	6	3.71	1.62
15 (Raft)	**14**	**30**	**2.00**	**15.00**
25	1	4	3.92	1.02
25	2	6	3.83	1.57
25	3	8	3.75	2.13
25 (Raft)	**24**	**50**	**2.00**	**25.00**

cluster scale and various amount of relay nodes. In the table, n is the number of nodes in the cluster, r refers to the number of relay nodes. Obviously when the number of relay nodes equals to the cluster scale, the Praft essentially the same as the original Raft algorithm, as highlighted in bold fonts in the table. $AML_L = 2r + 2$ and $AML_F = 2(n - r - 1)/(n - 1) + 2$ indicates the average message load that a leader and a follower handle a request, respectively. From the result, it is readily to observe that:

- In Praft, when the number of the relay nodes is the same, the extra message load brought by the increased cluster scale is evenly distributed to the leader node and relay nodes. For instance, when $n = 25$, the average message load ratio is 25 while the ratio becomes 1.02 when one relay node is joined, indicating that the relay node can effectively mitigate the load for a leader.
- For the cluster of the same scale (i.e., the same n), with more relay nodes, the load increases for a leader while decreases for a follower slightly.

Throughput with Various Cluster Sizes. Figure 4 depicts the comparison of throughput between Praft and etcd-raft. When the cluster scale is small, the message load is insufficient to make the leader node a bottleneck. The etcd-raft algorithm exhibits higher throughput since it needs two phases while Praft requires three phases. With the increase of the cluster scale, the throughput for etcd-raft significantly declines while our algorithm can realize about 135%−700% higher throughput, indicating the great efficiency and scalability improvement.

Latency Under Various Amount of Requests. As shown in Fig. 5, when $n = 5$, the latency is close between Praft and etcd-raft. With more requests from the client, etcd-raft exhibits higher latency. When $n = 15$, the difference of latency becomes larger due to the impact from both network scale and requests. In addition, with more relay nodes, the capability of handling requests in parallel increases, resulting smaller latency.

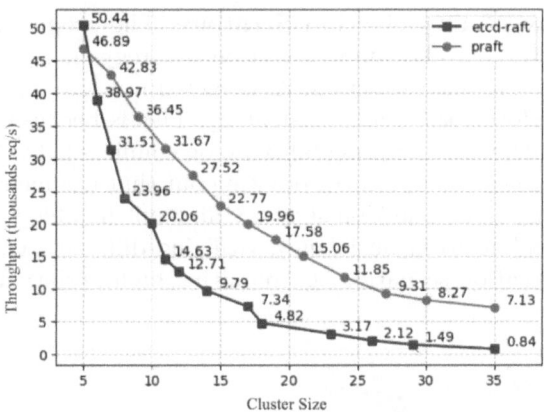

Fig. 4. The throughput comparison under different cluster scale.

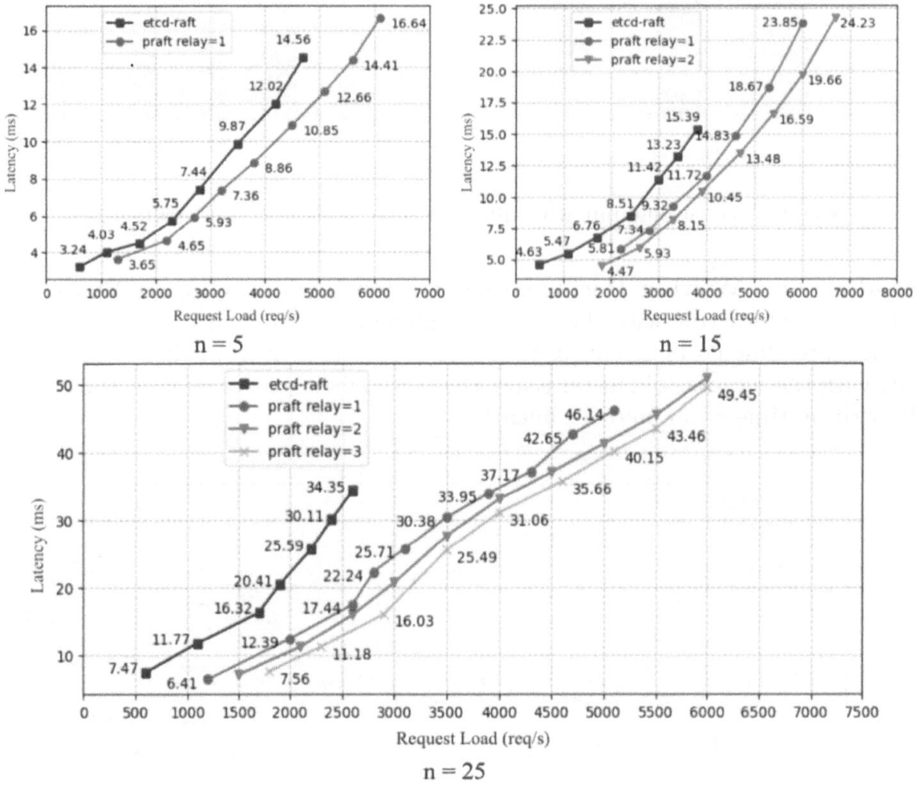

n = 5

n = 15

n = 25

Fig. 5. The comparison of latency under various amount of requests.

Impact of Relay Node Selection Strategy. The proposed Praft algorithm supports two types of relay node selection strategy, i.e., round robin-based dynamic selection and fixed selection. As depicted in Fig. 6, fixed selection strategy overall outperforms the dynamic strategy. This is because fixed relay nodes can considerably decrease the probability of log conflicts between the leader and the relay nodes. However, it is worth pointing out that if some relay nodes crash, then the fixed relay node selection strategy may not be able to select new relay nodes in time, leading to inconsistency. Utilizing different strategies hinges on the concrete application scenario, e.g., requiring high performance.

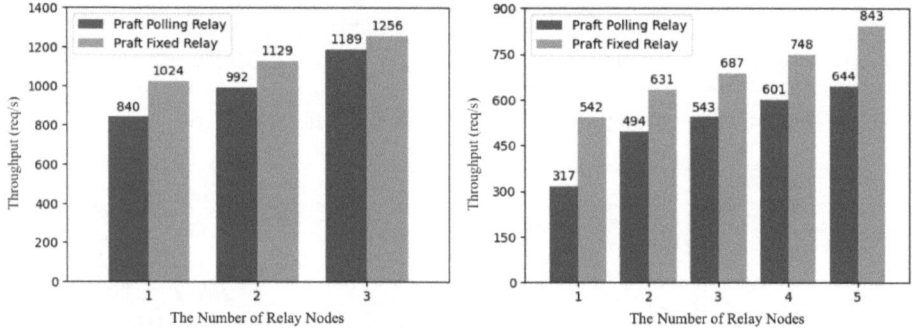

Fig. 6. The throughput with different relay node selection strategies.

Reading and Writing Performance Under Various Cluster Sizes. The operations interacting with the consensus include reading and writing. As shown in Fig. 7, reading costs much less than writing operations from clients. Additionally, with the increase of cluster scale, the reading time costs remain stable while the writing time costs increase linearly.

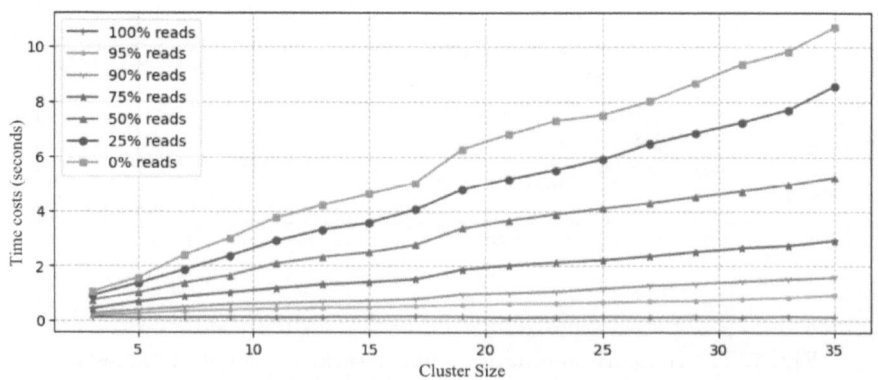

Fig. 7. The time costs of reading and writing operations via the consensus.

5 Conclusion

We propose a crash fault tolerant consensus algorithm, which is based on the popular raft algorithm yet with new designs aiming to improve raft's efficiency and scalability. Particularly, it is observed that the leader node in raft poses performance bottleneck, especially with the growth of cluster system scale. A relay mechanism is proposed to select multiple relay nodes to distribute the leader's message load. With a more layered architecture, a log conflict handling mechanism is presented ensure correctness and efficiency. Furthermore, a lease mechanism is introduced to efficiently handle the reading requests from the clients. Extensive experimental results demonstrate the feasibility and efficiency of the proposed consensus algorithm.

Acknowledgements. This work was supported in part by National Key R&D Project of China (No. 2023YFB3308600). Songlin He is also supported in part by NSFC (No. 62302403), the Fundamental Research Funds for the Central Universities (No. A0920502052301-186), and the New Interdisciplinary Cultivation Fund (No. YH15001124322133) with Southwest Jiaotong University, Sichuan, China.

References

1. Cachin, C., Vukolić, M.: Blockchain consensus protocols in the wild. arXiv preprint arXiv:1707.01873 (2017)
2. Castro, M., Liskov, B., et al.: Practical byzantine fault tolerance. In: OSDI, vol. 99, pp. 173–186 (1999)
3. Chen, X., He, S., Sun, L., Zheng, Y., Wu, C.: A survey of consortium blockchain and its applications. Cryptography **8**(2), 12 (2024)
4. Etcd-io: Raft library, November 2022. https://github.com/etcd-io/raft
5. Fu, W., Wei, X., Tong, S.: An improved blockchain consensus algorithm based on raft. Arab. J. Sci. Eng. **46**(9), 8137–8149 (2021)
6. Guo, B., Lu, Z., Tang, Q., Xu, J., Zhang, Z.: Dumbo: faster asynchronous BFT protocols. In: Proceedings of the 2020 ACM SIGSAC Conference on Computer and Communications Security, pp. 803–818 (2020)
7. He, S., et al.: Blockchain-based automated and robust cyber security management. J. Parallel Distrib. Comput. (2022)
8. He, S., Lu, Y., Tang, Q., Wang, G., Wu, C.Q.: Blockchain-based P2P content delivery with monetary incentivization and fairness guarantee. IEEE Trans. Parallel Distrib. Syst. **34**(2), 746–765 (2022)
9. He, S., et al.: Secure and efficient agreement signing atop blockchain and decentralized identity. In: Svetinovic, D., Zhang, Y., Luo, X., Huang, X., Chen, X. (eds.) BlockSys 2022. CCIS, vol. 1679, pp. 3–17. Springer, Singapore (2022). https://doi.org/10.1007/978-981-19-8043-5_1
10. He, S., Tang, Q., Wu, C.: Censorship resistant decentralized IoT management systems. In: Proceedings of the 15th EAI International Conference on Mobile and Ubiquitous Systems: Computing, Networking and Services, pp. 454–459 (2018)
11. He, S., Tang, Q., Wu, C.Q., Shen, X.: Decentralizing IoT management systems using blockchain for censorship resistance. IEEE Trans. Ind. Inform. 715–727 (2019)

12. Huang, D., Ma, X., Zhang, S.: Performance analysis of the raft consensus algorithm for private blockchains. IEEE Trans. Syst. Man Cybern. Syst. **50**(1), 172–181 (2019)
13. Kim, D., Doh, I., Chae, K.: Improved raft algorithm exploiting federated learning for private blockchain performance enhancement. In: 2021 International Conference on Information Networking, pp. 828–832. IEEE (2021)
14. Lamport, L.: Paxos made simple. ACM SIGACT News, 51–58 (2001)
15. Miller, A., Xia, Y., Croman, K., Shi, E., Song, D.: The honey badger of BFT protocols. In: Proceedings of the 2016 ACM SIGSAC Conference on Computer and Communications Security, pp. 31–42 (2016)
16. Nakamoto, S.: Bitcoin: a peer-to-peer electronic cash system (2008)
17. Ongaro, D., Ousterhout, J.: In search of an understandable consensus algorithm. In: 2014 USENIX Annual Technical Conference, pp. 305–319 (2014)
18. Wang, J., Li, Q.: Improved practical byzantine fault tolerance consensus algorithm based on raft algorithm. J. Comput. Appl. **43**(1), 122 (2023)
19. Wood, G., et al.: Ethereum: a secure decentralised generalised transaction ledger. In: Ethereum Project Yellow Paper, pp. 1–32 (2014)
20. Zhang, G., et al.: Reaching consensus in the byzantine empire: a comprehensive review of BFT consensus algorithms. ACM Comput. Surv. **56**(5), 1–41 (2024)
21. Zheng, P., Jiang, Z., Wu, J., Zheng, Z.: Blockchain-based decentralized application: a survey. IEEE Open J. Comput. Soc. **4**, 121–133 (2023)
22. Zhou, S., Ying, B.: VG-RAFT: an improved byzantine fault tolerant algorithm based on raft algorithm. In: 2021 IEEE 21st International Conference on Communication Technology, pp. 882–886. IEEE (2021)

Towards Pediatric Healthcare: A Blockchain-Based Framework for Transparent and Secure Medical Data Management

H. V. Khanh[1], T. D. Khoa[1], T. K. N. Ngan[2], V. C. P. Loc[1], N. H. Bang[1], N. T. Anh[1], N. N. Hung[1], and M. N. Triet[1]([⊠])

[1] FPT University, Can Tho city, Vietnam
{khanhvh,trietnm3}@fe.edu.vn
[2] FPT Polytecnic, Can Tho city, Vietnam

Abstract. The digitization of healthcare systems, particularly in pediatric care, presents both opportunities and challenges. Traditional Electronic Health Records (EHRs) improve certain healthcare processes but are hampered by significant issues related to data security, interoperability, and accessibility. This paper explores the integration of blockchain technology to address these vulnerabilities, offering a decentralized solution that enhances data integrity and security through cryptographic techniques and smart contracts. We introduce a blockchain-based framework tailored for pediatric healthcare, utilizing Non-Fungible Tokens (NFTs) to uniquely represent and manage each child's medical history. Our evaluation across four EVM-supported platforms—BNB, Fantom, Celo, and Polygon—demonstrates the framework's ability to deliver a secure, efficient, and cost-effective solution for managing pediatric medical records. The findings confirm the framework's adaptability and its potential to revolutionize pediatric healthcare data management by ensuring higher security standards and better accessibility.

Keywords: Pediatric Healthcare · Blockchain Technology · Electronic Health Records · Data Transparency · Interoperability · Non-Fungible Tokens · Decentralized Systems

1 Introduction

The healthcare sector, particularly pediatric care, is experiencing significant digital transformation. Traditional medical data management systems, while functional, exhibit considerable gaps in data security, interoperability, and accessibility—areas of critical importance in pediatric settings [4,20]. These challenges have led to the exploration of advanced technologies like the Internet of Healthcare Things (IoHT) and decentralized architectures, which are expected to fundamentally change the management of healthcare data [11,19]. Despite

J. Feng et al. (Eds.): ICBC 2024, LNCS 15425, pp. 95–108, 2025.
https://doi.org/10.1007/978-3-031-77095-1_7

the advancements brought by IoHT, which offers streamlined processes through microservice and brokerless architectures [10], pediatric healthcare still faces unique challenges due to the sensitivity of children's data. For instance, while Electronic Health Records (EHRs) have improved aspects of healthcare like diabetes screening [2], they also struggle with issues such as ineffective body mass index assessments [14].

EHRs bring many benefits to pediatric care, but they also face substantial challenges. These systems are often plagued by security vulnerabilities due to their centralized nature, risking unauthorized access and data manipulation [16]. Moreover, inconsistent interoperability across EHR systems complicates the smooth transfer of medical data, potentially leading to inaccuracies [17]). Blockchain technology is increasingly being regarded as a solution that can address these persistent issues [8]. Its decentralized structure prevents single points of failure and secures data integrity through advanced cryptographic techniques [5,18]. Smart contracts further enhance this system by providing standardized data exchange protocols, improving interoperability across platforms [6]. Additionally, the application of Non-Fungible Tokens (NFTs) within the blockchain framework allows for the unique representation of each child's medical history, enhancing control over data access and use by parents or guardians [12].

Our paper presents a blockchain-based framework specifically tailored for pediatric healthcare, designed to securely manage the capture, storage, and retrieval of children's medical records, ensuring both data integrity and ease of access [9]. We have conducted comprehensive evaluations of this system across four EVM-supported platforms (i.e., BNB, Fantom, Celo, and Polygon) to determine which offers the best combination of security, efficiency, and cost-effectiveness. The findings from these evaluations help substantiate the practical application of our proposed framework, confirming its adaptability and effectiveness across different blockchain infrastructures [15].

This paper is organized into six main sections, after the introduction, Sect. 2 reviews existing literature on the use of Electronic Health Records (EHRs) in pediatric care, highlighting the challenges related to data security, interoperability, and the potential of advanced technologies like blockchain to address these issues. In Sect. 3, we describe the architecture of our blockchain-based framework, detailing the integration of Non-Fungible Tokens (NFTs) and smart contracts to ensure secure and efficient management of pediatric health records. Section 4 presents the methodology and results of our comprehensive testing across four EVM-supported platforms—BNB, Fantom, Celo, and Polygon— to assess the framework's security, efficiency, and cost-effectiveness. Section 5 reflects on the findings, discussing the implications for pediatric healthcare and addressing potential threats to validity and limitations of the current framework. Finally, the conclusion summarizes the key outcomes of the research and proposes future directions for enhancing the scalability and applicability of the blockchain solution in diverse healthcare settings.

2   Related Work

2.1   Electronic Health Records in Child Healthcare

The integration of digital health technologies into pediatric care has significantly improved the accessibility and efficacy of services provided to young patients. One notable development has been the adoption of telehealth systems, which are particularly beneficial in enhancing the availability of healthcare for children residing in remote or underserved areas. Van Cleave et al. [20] highlighted the critical role of telehealth in providing necessary healthcare services to children with special healthcare needs who are located far from medical facilities. The implementation of EMRs has also been pivotal in streamlining pediatric health-care services. Choudhary et al. [2] explored how EMRs have facilitated adherence to diabetes screening protocols in children, ensuring timely and accurate management of childhood diabetes. This is essential for improving long-term health outcomes in pediatric diabetes care. Despite these benefits, EMRs face several challenges, particularly in ensuring comprehensive care for vulnerable groups such as children in foster care. Deans et al. [4] argued for a more integrated approach that combines EMRs with child welfare information systems to provide a more complete overview of the health status and needs of these children, thereby enhancing the availability and continuity of care.

Further demonstrating the utility of EMRs, Crosby et al. [3] successfully utilized these systems to manage home pain treatment for children suffering from sickle cell disease. Their strategy significantly reduced the necessity for emergency department visits by providing effective and accessible home-based care solutions, highlighting how digital records can directly contribute to reducing hospital admissions and improving patient management at home. Additionally, the accessibility of pediatric health data for both patients and their families has been a topic of keen interest and debate. Hagström et al. [7] investigated the perspectives of adolescents and their parents regarding access to Pediatric Electronic Health Records (PAEHRs). Their research uncovered mixed views on the balance between ensuring transparency in healthcare and maintaining the confidentiality of adolescent health information, emphasizing the complexity of access issues in pediatric health systems.

Overall, these studies underscore the pivotal role of digital health records in enhancing the availability and quality of healthcare for children, particularly in addressing the unique challenges faced by those in remote or vulnerable populations.

2.2   Advancements and Challenges of EHRs in Child Care

EHRs have become increasingly central to pediatric healthcare, facilitating improved operational efficiencies and potentially enhancing patient outcomes. Al-Shammari et al. [1] explored the effects of EHR implementation in a Pediatric Intensive Care Unit (PICU), where they noted not only enhanced operational efficiency but also a positive shift in healthcare providers' attitudes towards EHR adoption. This study illustrates the role of EHRs in making pediatric healthcare services more accessible by streamlining complex care processes. Despite these advancements, the effectiveness of EHRs in clinical practice often falls short of expectations. Shaikh et al. [14] highlighted a case where integrating automatic Body Mass Index (BMI) calculations into EHRs did not lead to improvements in weight assessments or nutritional counseling for children and adolescents. This example underscores the necessity for EHR systems to be accompanied by adequate training and effective implementation strategies to truly benefit pediatric care.

On a more positive note, targeted enhancements within EHR systems can lead to significant improvements in pediatric care. Saylam et al. [13] introduced an EHR alert designed to evaluate sleep quality in pediatric migraine patients using the Child and Adolescent Sleep Checklist (CASC). The implementation of this targeted alert significantly improved the identification of children with poor sleep habits, demonstrating how thoughtful modifications in EHR systems can make substantial differences in patient care. However, traditional EHR systems often face limitations, particularly in ensuring the continuity and security of pediatric health records. These systems can be fragmented, lack interoperability, and are frequently targeted by cybersecurity threats, which pose significant risks to sensitive child health information. The inherent limitations of current EHR systems highlight a critical need for innovative solutions that ensure both the availability and the security of health data.

The integration of blockchain technology, and specifically the use of NFTs, presents a promising avenue to address these challenges. NFTs can be employed to securely manage and track the ownership and history of electronic health records, offering an immutable and transparent framework. This approach not only enhances the security of pediatric health data but also improves its accessibility, ensuring that health records are easily transferable and accessible by authorized parties without compromising on privacy or data integrity. The motivation for adopting blockchain and NFTs in pediatric healthcare is driven by the need to overcome the significant limitations of current EHR systems, ensuring a more secure, efficient, and patient-centered approach to child healthcare management.

3 Methodology

3.1 Traditional Model for Pediatric Healthcare

Figure 1 illustrates the conventional process for managing pediatric medical tests and records in a healthcare setting. This workflow involves multiple stakeholders, including children, parents or guardians, nurses, doctors, medical laboratories, and drug stores, each playing a specific role in the patient care journey.

The process typically begins with nurses creating medical records for pediatric patients. These records serve as the foundation for tracking a child's health history and ongoing care. Parents or guardians, who are responsible for the

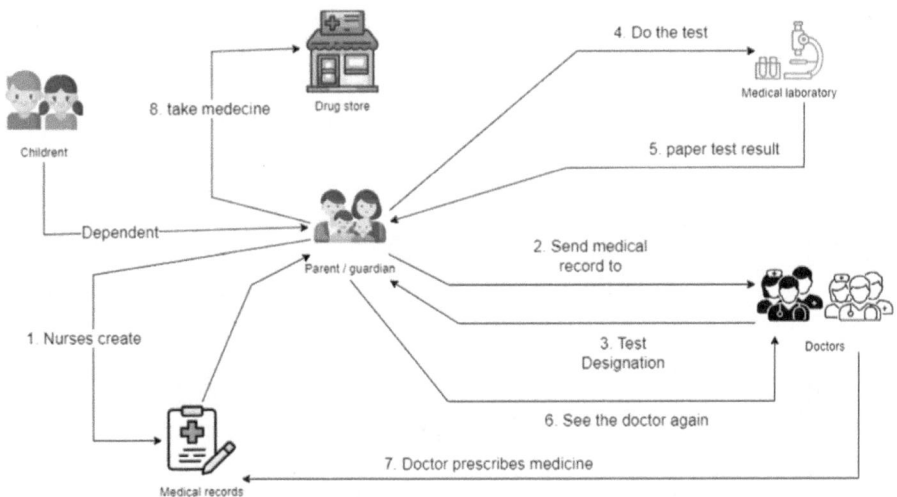

Fig. 1. Traditional Workflow for Pediatric Medical Testing and Record Management

child's wellbeing, are central to this workflow. They interact with various health-care providers and are the primary decision-makers and caretakers for the child's health needs. As the workflow progresses, second step are sent medical records to doctors for review and analysis. Based on their assessment, doctors may designate specific tests for the child. These tests are then conducted at a medical laboratory, where specialized equipment and expertise are available to perform the necessary diagnostic procedures. Once the tests are completed, the laboratory generates paper-based test results, which are then relayed back to the parent or guardian. Following the receipt of test results, parents often need to schedule another appointment to see the doctor again. During this follow-up visit, the doctor reviews the test results and, if necessary, prescribes medication for the child. This prescription is then taken to a drug store, where the parent or guardian can obtain the prescribed medicine for the child.

Throughout this process, there are multiple points of data exchange and decision-making. The workflow demonstrates the interdependencies between different healthcare providers and the central role of parents or guardians in managing their child's health. However, it also highlights potential inefficiencies in the system, such as the reliance on paper-based records and the need for multiple visits to different healthcare providers. These aspects of the traditional approach may present opportunities for improvement through the integration of digital technologies and more streamlined data management systems.

3.2 Blockchain-Based Pediatric Healthcare Architecture for Medical Test Records

Figure 2 presents a blockchain-based approach to managing pediatric healthcare records and processes. This system integrates various stakeholders and tech-

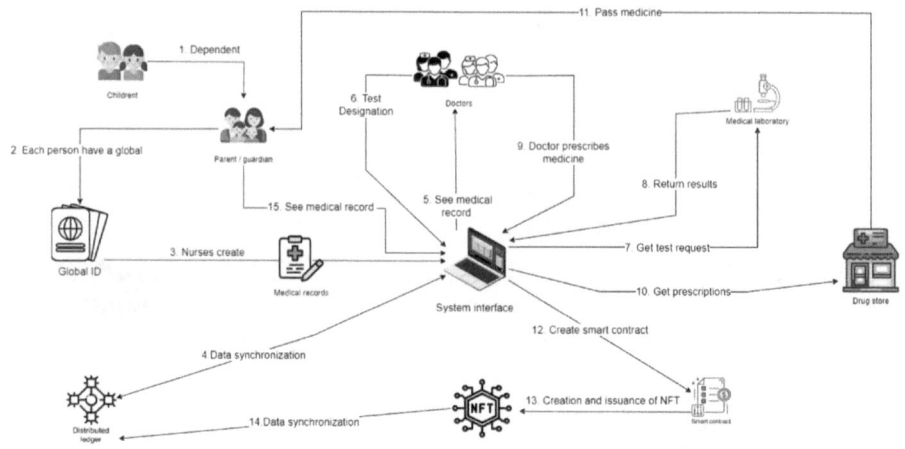

Fig. 2. Blockchain-Based Pediatric Healthcare Workflow

nologies to create a more interconnected and efficient workflow for managing children's medical information and test records. The process begins with the establishment of a dependent relationship between children and their parents or guardians. Each individual, including the child, is assigned a global ID, which serves as a unique identifier within the system. This global ID is a crucial element in ensuring that all medical records and interactions are correctly attributed and securely managed throughout the child's healthcare journey.

Nurses play a key role in initiating the digital record-keeping process by creating medical records for each child. These records are then entered into a centralized system interface, represented by a computer icon in the diagram. This interface acts as the primary point of interaction for various stakeholders, including medical professionals, laboratories, and pharmacies. It facilitates the flow of information and coordinates different aspects of the child's healthcare. The system interface is connected to a distributed ledger in the third step, which utilizes blockchain technology to ensure the security and immutability of the medical records. This ledger undergoes regular data synchronization with the central system, maintaining an up-to-date and tamper-resistant record of all healthcare interactions. The incorporation of blockchain technology adds a layer of transparency and trust to the record-keeping process, as all transactions and updates are recorded in a decentralized and verifiable manner.

As the child progresses through various medical procedures, the system continues to update and manage the information flow. Doctors can access medical records through the system interface to designate tests and prescribe medications. Medical laboratories receive test requests through the system and return results digitally, streamlining the process and reducing the risk of errors associated with paper-based systems. Prescriptions are electronically transmitted to drug stores, and the dispensing of medication is recorded in the system. Throughout these interactions, smart contracts are created to govern data access and usage, while NFTs are issued to represent unique medical records or test results. These digital assets are then synchronized with the distributed ledger, ensuring a secure and traceable record of all medical data and transactions related to the child's healthcare.

4   Evaluation

For the evaluation section of the paper focused on the use of blockchain technology for child's medical test EHRs, we consider the performance of the system across four EVM-supported platforms: BNB, Fantom, Celo, and Polygon. The choice of these platforms provides a diverse range of environmental settings, which helps in assessing the adaptability and efficiency of blockchain solutions under different network conditions and consensus mechanisms. The evaluation involves detailed analysis of three primary blockchain functions: transaction creation, NFT minting, and NFT transfer. These functions are critical as they directly relate to the core activities of handling medical test records on a blockchain, where transactions create records, NFT minting assigns ownership or certifies the records, and transfers enable the movement of these records between parties.

For each of these functions, we measure several key parameters to ensure a comprehensive evaluation of the blockchain implementation. These include the transaction fee, which is the cost incurred by users when executing transactions; the burn fee, which is a part of the transaction fee that is removed from circulation, influencing the economic model of the blockchain; gas used by the transaction, which reflects the computational resources required to process the transaction; and the gas price, which is the cost per unit of gas and fluctuates based on network demand. By analyzing these parameters, we can derive insights into the cost-effectiveness and resource efficiency of deploying blockchain for managing child medical records. This analysis not only helps in understanding the financial implications but also sheds light on the operational robustness of each platform under varying loads and transaction complexities.

The environments for the evaluation are set up to mirror typical use scenarios for medical records handling to ensure the results are relevant and applicable. The settings are configured to test the blockchain's performance during different levels of network activity and transaction volumes, providing a realistic view of how these platforms would perform in a real-world medical records management scenario. In this paper, the evaluation aims to offer a grounded understanding of how each blockchain platform can serve the needs of secure, efficient, and scalable management of child medical test records, without emphasizing overly optimistic or innovative attributes. This straightforward analysis is intended to assist decision-makers in assessing the viability and practicality of blockchain applications in healthcare contexts.

Table 1. Transaction fee

	Contract Creation	Create NFT	Transfer NFT
BNB Smart Chain	0.0273134 BNB ($18.66)	0.00109162 BNB ($0.75)	0.00057003 BNB ($0.39)
Fantom	0.00957754 FTM ($0.001)	0.000405167 FTM ($0.000)	0.0002380105 FTM ($0.000)
Polygon	0.006840710032835408 MATIC ($0.000)	0.000289405001852192 MATIC($0.000)	0.000170007501088048 MATIC($0.000)
Celo	0.007097844 CELO ($0.004)	0.0002840812 CELO ($0.000)	0.0001554878 CELO ($0.000)

4.1   Transaction Fee

The transaction fee data presented in Table 1 outlines the costs associated with performing key blockchain operations across four different EVM-supported platforms. These fees are critical for understanding the economic impact of deploying blockchain technology for handling medical test records. Starting with the BNB Smart Chain, we observe a significantly higher fee structure compared to the other platforms. For instance, the cost of contract creation is marked at $18.66, which is substantially higher than similar operations on Fantom, Polygon, and Celo. The fees for creating and transferring NFTs on BNB are $0.75 and $0.39, respectively. This suggests that while BNB Smart Chain offers robust support and infrastructure, it might come at a higher operational cost, which could be a limiting factor for its adoption in scenarios where cost efficiency is paramount.

In stark contrast, both Fantom and Polygon exhibit exceedingly low transaction costs, with fees for contract creation and NFT operations nearly negligible. For example, the cost of contract creation on Fantom is just $0.001, and similarly low on Polygon. Such low fees could make these platforms highly attractive for applications requiring high transaction volumes without significant financial outlay. This is particularly relevant in healthcare applications where frequent and numerous record updates are common. Celo also shows low transaction fees, with contract creation costing only $0.004, and even lower fees for NFT operations. This positions Celo as another feasible option for healthcare-related blockchain applications, combining reasonable cost with the capabilities of blockchain technology.

These variances in fee structures across the platforms highlight the trade-offs between cost and infrastructure capabilities. While BNB Smart Chain may offer more established services, its higher fees could be prohibitive for certain applications, unlike Fantom, Polygon, and Celo, which could provide more cost-effective solutions for managing child medical test records on the blockchain. This analysis should guide stakeholders in making informed decisions about which blockchain platform could best meet their specific needs in terms of both technical requirements and budget constraints.

4.2   Burn Fee

Table 2 on burn fees provides valuable insights into the costs associated with removing a portion of transaction fees from circulation—a practice that can

Table 2. Burn fee

	Contract Creation	Create NFT	Transfer NFT
BNB Smart Chain	0.00273134 BNB ($1.87)	0.000109162 BNB ($0.07)	0.00057003 BNB ($0.04)
Fantom	Do not mention	Do not mention	Do not mention
Polygon	0.00000000032835408 MATIC($0.01)	0.000000000001852192 MATIC($0.00)	0.000000000001088048 MATIC($0.00)
Celo	Do not mention	Do not mention	Do not mention

influence the economic stability and token supply of blockchain platforms. In this analysis, we focus on BNB Smart Chain and Polygon, as Fantom and Celo do not apply burn fees for the transactions listed.

For BNB Smart Chain, the burn fees associated with blockchain operations indicate a designed scarcity mechanism that may contribute to token value stability over time. The fee for contract creation is 0.00273134 BNB ($1.87), which, while modest, is significant enough to impact considerations for large-scale operations such as those in healthcare systems where numerous transactions can accumulate substantial costs. The fees for creating and transferring NFTs on BNB Smart Chain are relatively lower, at $0.07 and $0.04, respectively. These figures suggest a scaled approach where less complex transactions, like NFT transfers, incur lower burn fees, aligning the cost with the transaction's complexity and resource usage. Polygon's burn fees are extraordinarily low, with contract creation, NFT creation, and NFT transfer burn fees being close to negligible. For example, the burn fee for contract creation is a mere $0.01, and even lower for NFT operations. This almost inconsequential fee structure could make Polygon particularly appealing for applications where frequent and high-volume transactions are the norm, such as in digital record keeping in the medical sector.

The absence of burn fees on platforms like Fantom and Celo can also be noteworthy. The lack of burn fees might be part of a broader strategy to attract more transactions by lowering the overall cost for users. This could be particularly beneficial in environments where cost-effectiveness is crucial for scalability and mass adoption.

4.3 Gas Used by Transaction

Table 3. Gas Used by Transaction

	Contract Creation	Create NFT	Transfer NFT
BNB Smart Chain	2,731,340 (100%)	109,162 (100%)	57,003 (79.17%)
Fantom	2,736,440 (100%)	115,762 (100%)	68,003 (93.41%)
Polygon	2,736,284 (100%)	115,762 (100%)	68,003 (93.41%)
Celo	2,729,940 (76.92%)	109,262 (76.92%)	59,803 (69.8%)

Table 3 highlights the computational resources required for different types of transactions. Understanding these figures is crucial as they directly reflect the complexity and resource demands of the blockchain operations, impacting overall network performance and cost. For contract creation, all platforms, except Celo, show a consistent consumption of gas, with BNB Smart Chain, Fantom, and Polygon all using around 2.73 million units. This uniformity suggests that the contract creation operation is generally standardized in its complexity and resource usage across these platforms, reflecting a baseline level of efficiency in deploying new contracts on these blockchains.

Celo presents a different case with a lower gas usage of approximately 2.73 million units (76.92% of what is observed on the other platforms) for contract creation. This lower consumption could indicate a more optimized process for contract deployment on Celo, potentially reducing the costs and increasing the speed of operations, which is beneficial in environments where frequent updating of records, such as in medical databases, is required. When looking at the creation and transfer of NFTs, a similar pattern emerges. The gas used for creating NFTs is uniformly high across BNB Smart Chain, Fantom, and Polygon, with each consuming just over 115,000 units of gas. This consistency underscores the relatively fixed resource demands of NFT minting processes, irrespective of the underlying blockchain.

However, Celo again uses less gas for NFT creation, consuming only 76.92% of the gas compared to other platforms. This efficiency could make Celo an attractive option for applications involving extensive use of NFTs, such as securing medical records where each record could potentially be treated as an NFT for enhanced security and traceability. The NFT transfer process consumes less gas compared to contract creation and NFT minting, with BNB Smart Chain showing a notably lower usage at 57,003 units (79.17%). This suggests that transferring NFTs is less resource-intensive than creating them, which is advantageous for systems where NFTs need to be frequently transferred between parties, such as in healthcare systems where patient records might need to be accessed by various stakeholders.

4.4   Gas Price

Table 4. Gas Price

	Contract Creation	Create NFT	Transfer NFT
BNB Smart Chain	0.00000001 BNB (10 Gwei)	0.00000001 BNB (10 Gwei)	0.00000001 BNB (10 Gwei)
Fantom	0.0000000035 FTM (3.5 Gwei)	0.0000000035 FTM (3.5 Gwei)	0.0000000035 FTM (3.5 Gwei)
Polygon	0.000000002500000012 MATIC (2.500000012 Gwei)	0.000000002500000016 MATIC (2.500000016 Gwei)	0.000000002500000016 MATIC (2.500000016 Gwei)
Celo	0.0000000026 CELO (Max Fee per Gas: 2.7 Gwei)	0.0000000026 CELO (Max Fee per Gas: 2.7 Gwei)	0.0000000026 CELO (Max Fee per Gas: 2.7 Gwei)

Table 4 detailing gas prices across various transactions on BNB Smart Chain, Fantom, Polygon, and Celo reveals critical insights into the cost dynamics of executing blockchain operations on these platforms. Gas price, essentially the cost per unit of gas used, is a pivotal factor in determining the overall expense of blockchain transactions and can influence the choice of platform based on economic considerations.

BNB maintains a uniform gas price of 10 Gwei for all types of transactions, including contract creation, NFT creation, and NFT transfer. This consistency in gas pricing suggests a stable economic environment on the BNB Smart Chain, where users can predict and plan their transaction costs with certainty. However, compared to other platforms, this gas price is relatively higher, which could impact the overall cost-effectiveness of operations, especially in systems requiring high transaction throughput. Fantom displays the lowest gas price among the platforms analyzed, set at 3.5 Gwei for all transactions. This low cost could make Fantom an attractive platform for applications needing to manage large volumes of transactions efficiently and economically. For sectors like healthcare, where frequent and potentially numerous transactions (such as updates to medical records) are the norm, lower gas prices can significantly reduce operational costs.

Polygon offers a slightly higher gas price than Fantom, though still lower than BNB Smart Chain, at approximately 2.5 Gwei. This modest increase in price is likely a trade-off for the benefits offered by the Polygon network, such as enhanced scalability and speed. Such characteristics may justify the slightly higher costs, especially in applications where performance and rapid transaction processing are critical. Celo's gas price is comparably low, nearly aligning with Polygon's, and is set consistently for all transactions at around 2.7 Gwei. This indicates a cost-effective framework for executing transactions, which is crucial for maintaining the affordability of services deployed on the blockchain, particularly in cost-sensitive applications.

Our analysis of gas prices provides a foundational understanding of the economic considerations that must be weighed when selecting a blockchain platform. Each platform presents its own set of advantages and compromises between cost, stability, and performance. For instance, while BNB Smart Chain offers predictable pricing, it may not be the most cost-effective option for high-volume transactions. On the other hand, platforms like Fantom and Celo offer lower costs, potentially making them more suitable for applications where economic efficiency is a priority. This insight is essential for stakeholders in the healthcare sector or any field where blockchain technology is being considered for large-scale implementation.

5   Discussion

5.1   Our Findings

Our comprehensive evaluation of blockchain platforms for managing child medical test records has highlighted distinct characteristics in their economic and operational aspects. We found that while platforms like BNB Smart Chain provide robust support, they also come with higher transaction fees, which might not be viable for systems with high transaction frequencies such as healthcare databases. Conversely, platforms like Fantom and Polygon offer much lower transaction costs, making them potentially more suitable for healthcare applications due to their cost efficiency.

The analysis of burn fees brought to light BNB's higher fees which, while contributing to token value stability, might cumulatively impose significant costs in large-scale deployments. Polygon's negligible burn fees offer an advantage for frequent transactions that characterize the healthcare industry. This differentiation in burn fees underscores the economic trade-offs that must be considered when choosing a blockchain platform for healthcare applications. Furthermore, our analysis of gas usage and price revealed that while some platforms maintain a consistency across transactions, platforms like Celo provide a lower cost for operations, possibly due to more optimized processes. This efficiency could be particularly beneficial in healthcare settings where cost-effectiveness is crucial for scalability and widespread adoption.

5.2   Threats to Validity

One major threat to the validity of our findings is the variability in network conditions and transaction volumes that were not fully replicated in our test environments. Although we configured our evaluations to mirror typical usage scenarios for medical records handling, real-world conditions such as network congestion and fluctuating gas prices can significantly affect transaction costs and speeds. Additionally, our analysis was limited to only four blockchain platforms, which does not encompass the entire spectrum of available blockchain technologies. Each platform has unique underlying technologies and consensus mechanisms that might affect their suitability for specific applications. The generalization of our findings to other platforms should, therefore, be approached with caution.

5.3   Limitation

The primary limitation of this study is its focus on only a few selected blockchain platforms and specific transaction types. The blockchain landscape is vast and continuously evolving, with new platforms and technologies emerging that might offer improved performance or lower costs. Our study does not cover these newer or less common platforms, which could potentially provide better solutions for managing medical records. Moreover, the economic analysis was based on transaction fees, burn fees, gas usage, and gas prices at a snapshot in time. These metrics are subject to change due to factors like updates to network protocols or shifts in the blockchain's governance models, which could alter the cost-effectiveness and efficiency of these platforms in the future. This discussion section aims to provide a nuanced understanding of our findings while acknowledging the complexities and constraints that might affect their application in real-world scenarios. The choice of blockchain platform for healthcare or other critical sectors should be guided by careful consideration of both current and projected needs, balancing cost, efficiency, and scalability against the backdrop of an ever-evolving technological landscape.

6   Conclusion

The proposed blockchain-based framework represents a significant step forward in addressing the inherent limitations of traditional EHR systems in pediatric healthcare. By leveraging the decentralized nature of blockchain, enhanced with the unique capabilities of NFTs, our framework ensures robust data security and improved interoperability across different healthcare platforms. The comprehensive evaluation across multiple EVM-supported platforms has validated the framework's effectiveness in enhancing the security, efficiency, and cost-effectiveness of pediatric medical record management. As healthcare continues to evolve in the digital age, our blockchain solution stands out as a particularly suitable approach for enhancing the management of sensitive pediatric data. Future research should focus on expanding the adaptability of this framework to include more diverse healthcare environments and exploring further integration with emerging technologies to support the dynamic needs of pediatric care.

References

1. Al-Shammari, M.A.G., Yasir, A.A., Al-Doori, N.M.: Application of electronic medical record at intensive care unit in maternity and children hospital (2009)
2. Choudhary, D., Brown, B., Khawar, N., Narula, P., Agdere, L.: Implementation of electronic medical record template improves screening for complications in children with type 1 diabetes mellitus. In: Pediatric Health, Medicine and Therapeutics, pp. 219–223 (2020)
3. Crosby, L.E., et al.: Using quality improvement methods to implement an electronic medical record (EMR) supported individualized home pain management plan for children with sickle cell disease. J. Clin. Outcomes Manag. JCOM **21**(5), 210 (2014)
4. Deans, K.J., et al.: Health care quality measures for children and adolescents in foster care: feasibility testing in electronic records. BMC Pediatr. **18**, 1–11 (2018)
5. Duong-Trung, N., et al.: Multi-sessions mechanism for decentralized cash on delivery system. Int. J. Adv. Comput. Sci. Appl. **10**(9) (2019)
6. Ha, X.S., Le, T.H., Phan, T.T., Nguyen, H.H.D., Vo, H.K., Duong-Trung, N.: Scrutinizing trust and transparency in cash on delivery systems. In: Wang, G., Chen, B., Li, W., Di Pietro, R., Yan, X., Han, H. (eds.) SpaCCS 2020. LNCS, vol. 12382, pp. 214–227. Springer, Cham (2021). https://doi.org/10.1007/978-3-030-68851-6_15
7. Hagström, J., Blease, C., Haage, B., Scandurra, I., Hansson, S., Hägglund, M.: Views, use, and experiences of web-based access to pediatric electronic health records for children, adolescents, and parents: scoping review. J. Med. Internet Res. **24**(11), e40328 (2022)
8. Le, H.T., et al.: Patient-chain: patient-centered healthcare system a blockchain-based technology in dealing with emergencies. In: Shen, H., et al. (eds.) PDCAT 2021. LNCS, vol. 13148, pp. 576–583. Springer, Cham (2022). https://doi.org/10.1007/978-3-030-96772-7_54

9. Le, H.T., et al.: Bloodchain: a blood donation network managed by blockchain technologies. Network **2**(1), 21–35 (2022)
10. Nguyen, L.T.T., et al.: BMDD: a novel approach for IoT platform (broker-less and microservice architecture, decentralized identity, and dynamic transmission messages). PeerJ Comput. Sci. **8**, e950 (2022)
11. Nguyen, T.T.L., et al.: Toward a unique IoT network via single sign-on protocol and message queue. In: Saeed, K., Dvorský, J. (eds.) CISIM 2021. LNCS, vol. 12883, pp. 270–284. Springer, Cham (2021). https://doi.org/10.1007/978-3-030-84340-3_22
12. Quynh, N.T.T., et al.: Toward a design of blood donation management by blockchain technologies. In: Gervasi, O., et al. (eds.) ICCSA 2021. LNCS, vol. 12956, pp. 78–90. Springer, Cham (2021). https://doi.org/10.1007/978-3-030-87010-2_6
13. Saylam, E., Ramani, P., James, B., Savage, M., Jambhekar, S., Veerapandiyan, A.: Assessing sleep quality in children with migraines: implementation of electronic health record cue (s4. 005) (2022)
14. Shaikh, U., Nelson, R., Tancredi, D., Byrd, R.S.: Presentation of body mass index within an electronic health record to improve weight assessment and counselling in children and adolescents. Inform. Primary Care **18**(4) (2010)
15. Son, H.X., Carminati, B., Ferrari, E.: A risk assessment mechanism for android apps. In: 2021 IEEE International Conference on Smart Internet of Things (SmartIoT), pp. 237–244. IEEE (2021)
16. Son, H.X., Chen, E.: Towards a fine-grained access control mechanism for privacy protection and policy conflict resolution. Int. J. Adv. Comput. Sci. Appl. **10**(2) (2019)
17. Son, H.X., Hoang, N.M.: A novel attribute-based access control system for fine-grained privacy protection. In: Proceedings of the 3rd International Conference on Cryptography, Security and Privacy, pp. 76–80 (2019)
18. Son, H.X., et al.: Towards a mechanism for protecting seller's interest of cash on delivery by using smart contract in hyperledger. Int. J. Adv. Comput. Sci. Appl. **10**(4) (2019)
19. Thanh, L.N.T., et al.: IOHT-MBA: an internet of healthcare things (IOHT) platform based on microservice and brokerless architecture. Int. J. Adv. Comput. Sci. Appl. **12**(7) (2021)
20. Van Cleave, J., Stille, C., Hall, D.E.: Child health, vulnerability, and complexity: use of telehealth to enhance care for children and youth with special health care needs. Acad. Pediatr. **22**(2), S34–S40 (2022)

SoK on Blockchain Evolution and Taxonomy

Thuat Do[1]($\boxtimes$) and Dinh-Ngoc Bui[2]

[1] Department of Mathematics, Hong Kong University of Science and Technology,
Hong Kong, China
thuat86@gmail.com
[2] Rivalz Network, Hanoi, Vietnam

Abstract. This paper, based on the well-known problems and the most technical challenges in Blockchain space, studies ground-breaking and critical inventions of various blockchain protocols to give a taxonomy for the evolution of four public Blockchain generations. The first and second generations are well-defined by Bitcoin and Ethereum, respectively. The latest state-of-the-art blockchain protocols have been shaping the third and fourth generations, by their own outstanding innovations and distinguished architectural designs to solve limited capacity and scalability of Bitcoin and Ethereum. This work helps readers quickly capture historical evolution and innovations of public blockchains, envisioning the next advancements of Web3 as well as the Internet of Value (Internet 2.0).

Keywords: Blockchain · Bitcoin · distributed ledger technology (DTL) · Ethereum · Internet of Money · Web3

1 Introduction

This section provides a literature review on blockchain classification and taxonomy, both scientific publications and non-academic articles. It also summarizes the most important contribution of the paper and research method. Section 2 extensively presents major problems and challenges of public blockchains, their innovation and evolution, then introduces a taxonomy of four public blockchain generations. Section 3 concludes the work with application of our taxonomy on popular public chains.

1.1 A Literature Review

Blockchain has been broadly recognized as a breakthrough technology of the world. Web3 refers to the next generation of Internet applications based on blockchain protocols, envisioning *the Internet of Money* (termed by Andreas M. Antonopoulos [1] in his book with the same title) to store and transfer value. Alternatively, some authors [2,3] introduced and defined the concepts

© The Author(s), under exclusive license to Springer Nature Switzerland AG 2025
J. Feng et al. (Eds.): ICBC 2024, LNCS 15425, pp. 109–120, 2025.
https://doi.org/10.1007/978-3-031-77095-1_8

of *Internet of Value*, discussed how blockchain technologies connect and change businesses.

In the academic field, many scientists have extensively investigated Blockchain. Under the views of system architects, X. Xu et al. [20], in 2017, proposed a taxonomy capturing significant architectural characteristics of blockchains and the impact of their principal designs which are useful for architectural considerations on the performance and quality attributes of blockchain-based systems. In 2019, Paolo Tasca [17], from bottom-up, deconstructed blockchains into their building blocks, then hierarchically classified into main and sub-components to identify and compare. Then, under technical view, a taxonomy tree is introduced across different blockchain architectural configurations.

Shehu M.S. et al. [26], in 2018, used existing methods in information systems to develop a classification regarding blockchain platforms. Olga Labazova et al. [18], in 2019, and Sam G. et al. [19], in 2020, classified applications of Blockchain technologies in various industries and domains. Omer F. Cangir et al. [25], in 2021, proposed categorization for blockchain based distributed storage technologies, then used the taxonomy to compare and evaluate various solutions.

Considering consensus as the heart of any blockchain, in 2019, Shehar Bano et al. [21] proposed a systematic framework to study blockchain consensus mechanisms, their security and performance properties. In 2020, Sarah Bouraga [22] reviewed and analyzed 28 consensus protocols, then comprehensively categorized them under a framework of origin, design, performance and security. Jeff Nijsse [23] and Garay J. et al. [24] also proposed taxonomy for consensus mechanisms.

In the articles of Stephan Cummings (Feb 2019), Ruchika Dubey (Sep 2019), Kirsty Moreland (May 2021), Nathan Reiff (Sep 2021), Willigut (Oct 2022), The Nation Thailand (Nov 2022), the writers had various attempts to classify public blockchain generations. They almost agree on the 1st and 2nd generations, while having a controversy on the 3rd and the next ones. However, there was a lack of scientific research methods in those mentioned articles. This paper proposes a taxonomy for the evolutionary generations of public blockchains.

1.2   Research Method

The author studies the evolution of Blockchain under historical points of view, hence finds out what problems and challenges are significant to motivate innovations, what inventions are breaking to shape a new chapter for advancements of Blockchain Technology. More explicitly, instead of digging into consensus mechanisms, application perspectives or deep technology designs of blockchain protocols, the author considers the following criteria to categorize blockchains, to classify four evolutionary generations of public blockchains.

– Development history;
– Major problems addressed to solve (e.g. digital cash system, decentralized settlement, scalability, Blockchain Trilemma, high performance, cross-chain interoperability, composability);

– System architecture and technological designs: network layer, consensus, virtual machine, application-oriented modularity, etc.

2 Four Public Blockchain Generations

2.1 Bitcoin and the 1st Blockchain Generation

Hash function, Merkle tree [6,7], block-chaining design of David Chaum[1] [8] and public key cryptography (e.g. Elliptic Curve Digital Signature Algorithm) are primitive materials for Satoshi Nakamoto[2] to create Bitcoin, the first practical blockchain network in the world. Bitcoin's whitepaper [4] was publicly available in 2008 at the website www.bitcoin.org and Bitcoin mainnet went live on 3 January 2009. The Bitcoin Whitepaper entitled *"Bitcoin: A Peer-to-Peer Electronic Cash System"*, and in the Bitcoin's genesis block, the first coinbase transaction messaged the string *"The Times 03/Jan/2009 Chancellor on brink of second bailout for banks"* mentioning the title of an article on The Times of London admit 2008–2009 financial crisis in U.K, U.S and several developed nations caused by failure of centralized bank systems. By inventing Bitcoin, Satoshi Nakamoto made critical dedications to the world.

1. He orchestrated designs of distributed system, immutable data structure and cryptography techniques in a single software (i.e. Bitcoin core).
2. He introduced Nakamoto Consensus, the first and the most popular Proof of Work (PoW) consensus algorithm in the Blockchain space.
3. He introduced a tamper-proof ledger architecture (the first replicated state machine of the world).
4. He realized the concept of electronic cash system, more explicitly, cryptography currency (or cryptocurrency), together with the concept of token economics (or tokenomics) based on game theory.
5. Satoshi Nakamoto fathered the philosophy of decentralized system and decentralized governance which contrasts to centralized entities.

Bitcoin, as the first blockchain network, has become the philosophy and technology fundamentals for all the following blockchain platforms, including Ethereum. Bitcoin, as the first cryptocurrency, has been becoming the **digital gold** of the world, a miracle in the 21st century, and potentially reshaping global money and financial systems. Readers can find more about Bitcoin in [1]. The historical origin and variations of blockchain technology is surveyed in [5] by Sherman, Alan T et al. (2019).

The 1st generation remarked on Bitcoin's birthday on 3 Jan 2009, noting its mainnet launch date - the genesis block. The followers are XRP[3] (launched 2 June 2012), Dogecoin (launched 6 December 2013), Stellar - XLM (launched

---

[1] David Chaum is credited as the godfather of cryptocurrency. He introduced the first digital currency in 1995 but failed in practice.

[2] Pseudonym of an anonymous programmer or an unknown group of cryptographers.

[3] XRP is formerly called XNS, a cryptocurrency affiliated with Ripple Labs.

31 July 2014), utilized Byzantine Fault Tolerance (BFT) consensus to develop digital currency for banking and financial sector. Litecoin (mainnet launched 13 October 2011), Bitcoin Cash (launched 1 August 2017), Dogecoin (launched 6 December 2013), all aiming to build corresponding crypto-currencies (alternatively, digital currencies) generated and kept by distributed ledger technologies as introduced and visioned by Bitcoin and its creator - Shatoshi Nakamoto. These cryptocurrencies aim to solve against the centralized, nontransparent control problem of fiat currencies and bank systems, then heading to the future of money which is decentralized, transparent and censorship resistant, backed by community and built for community.

2.2   The 2nd Blockchain Generation

The 2nd generation refers to blockchains proposed to solve two major problems: **privacy transactions** and **programmable money**. Dash[4] (launched 18 January 2014), Monero (18 April 2014), Zcash (28 October 2016) are designed to hide the mapping between senders and receivers, hence offering transaction privacy in contrast to Bitcoin and the 1st blockchain generation.

Programmable money and decentralized applications are not available on Bitcoin and cryptocurrency networks based on scripting languages. Vitalik Buterin (born 1994) had a ground-breaking approach with Blockchain Technology as he conceived and founded Ethereum in 2013, (visit his vision in Ethereum Whitepaper). Ethereum mainnet launched on 30 July 2015, introduced a Turing-complete platform to enable arbitrary smartcontract implementation and application programming on top of blockchain which was impossible and regarding Bitcoin, Dash, XRP, Stellar and others at that time. Vitalik Buterin and Ethereum Foundation's Imaginations were a breakthrough in the Blockchain evolution, overhauling Bitcoin Core, inventing and paving the development way for the most important concepts in the Blockchain Space: smartcontract platform, tokenization, tokenomics, decentralized finance (DeFi) & stable-coins, decentralized autonomous organization (DAO), decentralized file storage, decentralized data feed (oracle), etc. Turing-completeness on blockchain, Ethereum Virtual Machine (EVM) and Solidity language, were outstanding inventions of Ethereum developers dedicated to the Blockchain space. Additionally, Ethereum used Ethash-PoW algorithm, protecting the network against ASIC-mining, an issue on Bitcoin and its hard-forked networks.

Up to now, almost public blockchains are smartcontract platforms equipped Turing-completeness. Such typical examples after Ethereum are Cardano (September 2017), EOS (June 2018), Tron Network (July 2018), Polygon (June 2020), BNB Chain[5] (September 2020).

---

[4] It was named Xcoin at launch, then Darkcoin.

[5] It was re-branded in February 2022 from Binance Chain and Binance Smart Chain - BSC. Binance Chain is based on Tendermint Core but no runtime environment (VM). It is now the beacon of BNB Chain, while BSC is the EVM-chain, making BNB Chain a multi-chain system.

Currently, Ethereum is still the leading smartcontract platform in terms of developers & user communities, application diversity, DeFi prosperity and composability. EVM is the most popular runtime environment for smartcontracts, and Solidity is the most smartcontract programing language[6].

With a distinct approach, IOTA (launched 11 July 2016) introduced a Tangle protocol based on DAG, targeting a cryptocurrency network oriented for IoT devices and their applications, with theoretically unbounded scale. However, applications of IOTA are very limited due to asynchronicity and no virtual machine.

Essentially, the 2nd generation was noticed by Ethereum and the emergence of Turing-complete blockchains (i.e. **smartcontract platforms**). Such blockchains have gained plentiful applications and wide range of adoption, while privacy-supported chains (alternatively, privacy coins, as mentioned, Dash, Monero, Zcash) and non-Turing-complete chains have not. The impact and adoption of privacy coins have been going down due to limited applications and regulatory concerns.

2.3   The 3rd Blockchain Generation

The 3rd generation attempted to solve the problems of Bitcoin and Ethereum smartcontract platform: **scalability** and the **Blockchain Trilemma**. In the past years, PoW-based Ethereum normally processed 14 transactions per seconds (TPS), congestion and gas spikes often happened on the network. Scalability and gas efficiency became the biggest challenge and concern for blockchain developers during 2016–2018. Scalability indicates the ability of a blockchain to process more transactions when adding computing resources. This is very limited (even nearly impossible) for Bitcoin and Ethereum.

Many projects, Cardano mainnet launched in September 2017, EOS launched in June 2018, Tron Network launched in July 2018, proposed to build Turing-complete blockchains, smartcontract platforms with better performance and scale, then killing Ethereum. They invented novel consensus mechanisms based on Proof of Stake (PoS) to replace energy-consuming PoW and to enable scaling, accompanied with innovations on architectural designs and virtual machines. Cardano developed PoS Ouroboros [10] and built a Turing-complete language on top of UTXO assets, white EOS and Tron both implemented Delegated Proof of Stake (DPOS) with 21 and 27 validators, offering much higher performance compared to Ethereum, respectively. Hedera introduced a public, permissioned ledger protocol (as an alternative to blockchain) based on the invention of Hashgraph (non-linear) architecture and asynchronous BFT (aBFT) consensus. Hedera mainnet launched on 14 August 2018, claiming it can process around 10k TPS with ability to scale more. Polygon (formerly named Matic Network), launched in June 2020, proposed to scale Ethereum as a sidechain solution (or layer-2 scaling)

---

[6] Solidity was created by Gavin James Wood (or Gavin Wood), cofounder of Ethereum, chief architect of EVM. It is mostly used to implement smartcontracts on Ethereum and EVM-compatible platforms like Tron, BNB Chain, Polygon.

based on Plasma Bridge. Now, Tron and Polygon have plenty of applications and wide adoption, the ability to process up to thousands TPS. On the other hand, EOS platform is complete with many merits in technology fundamentals but lacks applications due to the conflict between EOS community and Blockone (the initial developer of EOS). Cardano has PoS-Ouroboros consensus [10] as its most important innovation, but it is incomplete, with limited development tools for smartcontract implementation and application deployment. UTXO model results in difficulties to build a VM. Haskell, the language to develop Cardano and to build contracts on its top, is also unfamiliar to the developer community.

The Blockchain Trilemma was the most notable problem during 2018–2020, termed by Vitalik Buterin, raising the *"decentralization, security, scalability"* triangle which is difficult to balance among those triple. It was an observation from Hedera, EOS, Tron and other projects offering higher performance than Ethereum but somehow sacrificing decentralization. More accurately, the Triangle is decentralization, safety, scalability, according to S. Leonardos et al. [15]. In the paper, the authors explicitly introduced *PREStO*, a formal and systematic framework to assess blockchain consensus protocols under five axes: *optimality, stability, efficiency, robustness, and persistence.* Figure 1 presents a visual representation of the Blockchain Trilemma in relation to the PREStO framework. The trade-off between safety, scalability and decentralization is precisely captured by the corresponding subcategories in optimality, efficiency and stability. Robustness and persistence offer alternative approaches for a long-term resolution of the Trilemma.

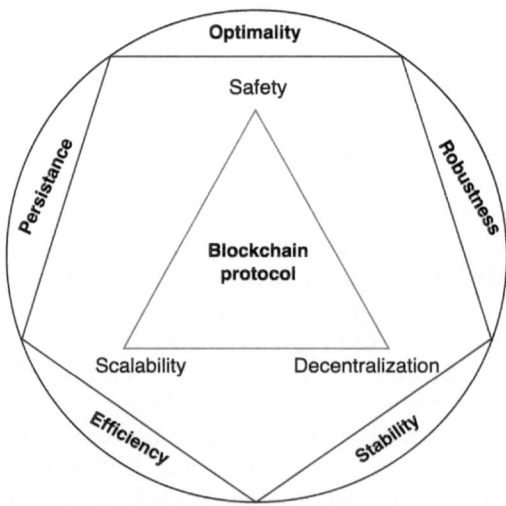

Fig. 1. Blockchain Trilemma in relation to the PREStO framework.

– Figure 2 presents a dealing with the Blockchain Trilemma: The green dot denotes an ideal protocol that satisfies all three properties (safety, decen-

tralization, and scalability) in equilibrium. The blue dot denotes a protocol that cycles around the ideal solution and which satisfies the incompatible properties in a weakly persistent (recurrent) manner.
– Scalability and decentralization are often held back by safety, but safety tends to be compromised by any shift on a network that offers scalability.
– Projects either choose to focus on two out of three or work on finding a solution to tackle the Trilemma once and for all.
– Finding a balance between the three properties is very difficult. However, a *good-enough* solution to the problem could lead to greater adoption of cryptocurrency and Blockchain and a wide-spread use of the technology across industries and the globe.

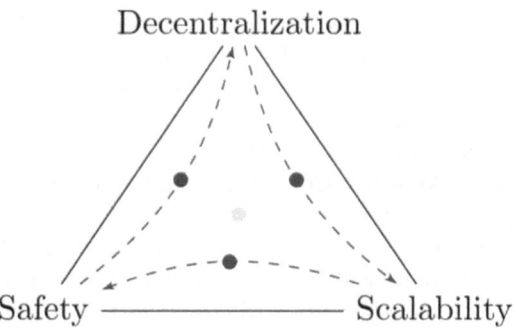

Fig. 2. Dealing with Blockchain Trilemma

Silvio Micali, a scientist at MIT, founded Algorand (mainnet launched in June 2019), claimed to solve the Blockchain Trilemma by inventions of a Pure Proof of Stake (PPoS) consensus and a verifiable random function (VRF). Although Silvio Micali stated that his team could boost Algorand to 46000 transaction per second (TPS), according to Algorand 2021 Performance report, Algorand throughput (average 1300, max 6000 TPS) at present is rather similar to Tron, EOS, Polygon. Audiences can refer to Mauro Conti et al. [14] presenting a security analysis of Algorand and an attack scenario by exploiting a security flaw in the messages validation process of the Byzantine Agreement.

Overall, although a candidate for The Blockchain Trilemma is not yet acknowledged widely, radical innovations of the 3rd generation is very significant to advance Blockchain Technology and to bring extensive applications and usecases to the Blockchain and cryptocurrency space, heading to mainstream adoption in the future. The 3rd generation are remarked by innovations of PoS and DPoS consensus mechanisms, hashgraph design and sharding technologies, all implying better performance than Ethereum.

2.4   The 4th Blockchain Generation

The fourth generation continues to deal with scalability, targets high performance blockchains, and also raises a new big challenge in cross-chain communication and application-custom flexibility.

High performance blockchain is another approach to the scaling problem, firstly introduced in commercial production by Solana (Mar 2020), then followed by Aptos. They aimed to build monolithic chains with high throughput (measured by TPS) and fast finality (i.e. low latency). Their developers claim they can build such single and linear chains to reach tens of thousand TPS and few-second finality. In Solana Whitepaper [9], Anatoly Yakovenko said that the protocol can reach up to 71000 TPS thanks to a deterministic block producer selection mechanism, Proof of History and Tower BFT consensus. Rati Gelashvili et al. [13] presents Block-STM, a parallel execution engine for smartcontracts, running in production on Aptos, which helps the chain achieves up to 110k tps in the Diem benchmarks and up to 170k tps in the Aptos benchmarks. SUI blockchain has the same fundamentals as Aptos. Unfortunately, in some way, they traded off security (more explicitly safety and liveness) and/or decentralization for high throughput. People have observed 11 times of outage on Solana since its beta mainnet launch on 16 March 2020. Aptos, mainnet launched on 12 October 2022, currently has 145 active validators and recorded peaks of around 8400 TPS. SUI, mainnet launched on 3 May 2023, currently has 106 SUI-validators. Solana better has 1505 SOL-validators. However, all the three blockchains are far less decentralized than Ethereum with 1054866 ETH-validators, recorded on 6 August 2024.

Sharding technology is an important solution to deal with scalability and high performance, which partitions a large database and a blockchain network into many shards to multiply performance. Readers refer to Gang Wang et al. [27] for a systematic and comprehensive review on sharding techniques and protocols. Zilliqa (mainnet launched on 31 January 2019), Near Protocol (22 April 2020), and TON - Telegram Open Network (May 2021) are frontiers among sharding protocols. Sharding protocols are supposed to be promising for great numbers of TPS (up to 100k TPS and more). After The Merge successfully executed on 15 September 2022, transitioned Ethereum to PoS consensus mechanism, Blockchain communities are waiting for Ethereum 2.0 with sharding upgrades. All sharding chains require a special chain at the center to govern and coordinate all other shards. They can be considered as *homogeneous multi-chain systems*, contrasting with *heterogeneous multi-chain systems* in the following.

Cross-chain interoperability is one among major problems and big challenges of Blockchain technology. By sovereignty, each chain is separated and isolated from all others. Simply speaking, it is impossible to move bitcoin on Bitcoin Network to Ethereum (i.e. asset transfer from a chain to another). More generally, how to make different blockchains communicate and interoperate with each other?

Cosmos (mainnet launched on 13 March 2019), Polkadot (launched 26 May 2020), by radically outstanding inventions, are pioneers to propose *heteroge-*

neous multi-chain systems, for which a special chain at the center governs and coordinates all other chains (built on a standardized framework) in the system. This architecture allows triple-addressing scalability, cross-chain interoperability, and customization for various application-purposed chains. Cosmos has a Cosmos Hub and zones based on Tendermint BFT consensus [30] and Inter-Blockchain Communication (IBC) protocol. Polkadot has a Relay Chain and parachains built on BABE-GRANDPA consensus [11,12]. Avalanche (launched 21 September 2020), Internet Computer Protocol - ICP (launched on 7 May 2021) then follows with their distinguished innovations. Avalanche invented a hybrid architecture of DAG and linear ledgers, of UTXO assets and account model, powered by Snowman - a novel leaderless BFT consensus [29] which could handle 4500 TPS on multiple subnets. ICP is built on Chain-key cryptography derived from threshold BLS signatures, multi-subnet architecture governed by a Network Nervous System, and Motoko smartcontract language. With a novel BFT consensus [28] derived from chain-key technology, ICP mainnet handles peaks of 24235 TPS normally, and theoretically scale infinitely with every application feasibly hosted onchain. Following the multi-chain direction, BNB Chain, Tron Network and Klaytn have been upgrading and transforming to heterogeneous multi-chain systems since early 2022.

3   Discussion

Although people still debate on a possible solution for The Blockchain Trilemma, advancement in the space is fast with bundles of groundbreaking innovations and initiatives. We observed and analyzed the most significant criteria and characterizations to classify four public blockchain generations, addressed the most significant problems and protocols solving them, corresponding with their consensus type and groundbreaking inventions. In Table 1, among blockchain protocols, we give typical examples and their performance: real TPS (TPS) observed on mainnet, time to transaction finality (TTF) or latency. Performance is difficult to measure and there is a confusion between performance versus scalability (see J. Bonneau [16]). Additionally, records on TPS and TTF may vary over different times of observations. They are supplementary, not critical in this paper. Table 2 gives typical examples of smartcontract platforms of the 3rd generation.

To conclude the paper, the author applies proposed categorization and taxonomy to briefly classify popular public blockchain platforms on the Top of Coinmarketcap. The classifying characteristics and examples are useful for readers to apply for their own cases. It is worthy to note that some platforms have been evolving with many planned upgrades in the future, hence they may overlap in several generations (examples in Tables 1, 2). Since 2022, layer-2 and layer-3 based on optimistic and zero-knowledge roll-up technologies have been emerging as a promising scaling solution for Ethereum, possibly leading any underlying settlement blockchains (i.e. Layer-1 s) to a multi-chain systems with scalability and customizability. Since most layer-2 blockchains are universal-purpose smartcontract platforms for scale, they can be considered belonging to the 3rd generation. We will investigate layer-2 evolution in the next research.

Table 1. A summary on four generations of public blockchains

Gens	Problems	Platforms	Inventions	TPS	TTF
1st	P2P settlement	Bitcoin 2009	Nakamoto PoW	7	60 m
	Censorship-resistant		Decen. ledger & economics		
2nd	Turing-completeness	Ethereum 2015	Ethash PoW, PoS	15	6 m
	Smartcontract/Dapps		EVM & Solidity	25	6 m
3rd	Scale	Hedera 2018	DAG Hashgraph, aBFT	3k	6 s
	Scale	Tron 2018	DPoS, TronVM	300	36 s
	Blockchain Trilemma	Algorand 2019	Pure PoS & VRF	6k	4 s
4th	Interoperation	Cosmos 2019	Tendermint BFT & IBC	1k	7 s
	Interoperation	Polkadot 2020	BABE-GRANDPA PoS	1k	60 s
	High performance	Solana 2020	PoH & TowerBFT	8k	1 s
	High performance	TON 2021	Sharding & TonVM	5k	6 s
	High performance	Aptos, SUI	MOVE & MoveVM	8k	1 s
	Scale & Interoperation	Avalanche 2020	Hybrid ledger, SnowmanBFT	1k	3 s
	Scale & Interoperation	ICP 2021	ChainKey BFT, Motoko	24k	1 s

Table 2. The 3rd generation, layer-1 smartcontract platforms (some are evolving to heterogeneous multi-chain systems)

Platforms	Ledger	type	Governance	Consensus	VM	Architecture
BNB Chain	account	linear	Permissioned	PoSA	EVM	heterogeneous
Cardano	UTXO	linear	Permissionless	PoS		monolithic
Hedera	account	DAG	Permissioned	BFT		monolithic
VeChain	account	linear	Permissioned	PoA	EVM	monolithic
Fantom	account	linear	Permissionless	BFT-PoS	EVM	monolithic
Theta	account	linear	Permissionless	PoS	EVM	monolithic
EOS	account	linear	Permissionless	DPoS	WASM	monolithic
Tezos	account	linear	Permissionless	PoS	TezosVM	monolithic
Flow	account	linear	Permissionless	PoS	FlowVM	monolithic
Klaytn	account	linear	Permissionless	PoS	EVM	heterogeneous
Casper	account	linear	Permissionless	PoS	CasperVM	monolithic
Oasis	account	linear	Permissionless	PoS	EVM, Ewasm	monolithic
Chiliz	account	linear	Permissioned	PoSA	EVM	monolithic

References

1. Antonopoulos, A.M., Hariry, S.H.E., Lords, M.K., Morgan, P., Scothorn, M., Zolt-Gilburne, S.: The Internet of Money: Talks by Andreas M. Antonopoulos, Merkle Bloom LLC (2016)

2. Vadgama, N., Jiahua, X., Tasca, P.: Enabling the Internet of Value: How Blockchain Connects Global Businesses. Springer, Cham (2022). https://doi.org/10.1007/978-3-030-78184-2

3. Treiblmaier H.: Defining the internet of value. In: Vadgama N., Xu J., Tasca P. (eds.) Enabling the Internet of Value: Future of Business and Finance, pp. 3–10. Springer, Cham (2022). https://doi.org/10.1007/978-3-030-78184-2_1

4. Nakamoto, S.: Bitcoin: a peer-to-peer electronic cash system (2008)

5. Sherman, A.T., Farid, J., Haibin, Z., Enis, G.: On the origins and variations of blockchain technologies. IEEE Secur. Priv. **17**(1), 72–77 (2019). https://doi.org/10.1109/MSEC.2019.2893730

6. Bayer, D., Haber, S., Stornetta, W.S.: Improving the efficiency and reliability of digital time-stamping. In: Capocelli R., De Santis A., Vaccaro U. (eds.) Sequences II. Springer, New York (1993). https://doi.org/10.1007/978-1-4613-9323-8_24

7. Merkle R.C.: Secrecy, authentication, and public-key systems, PhD Thesis, Stanford University (1979)

8. Chaum, D.L.: Computer Systems Established, Maintained, and Trusted by Mutually Suspicious Groups, PhD Thesis, University California, Berkely (1982)

9. Yakovenko, A.: Solana Whitepaper (2020)

10. , Bernardo, D., Gazi, P., Kiayias, A., Russell, A.: Ouroboros praos: an adaptively-secure, semi-synchronous proof-of-stake blockchain. In: Nielsen, J., Rijmen, V. (eds.) Advances in Cryptology - EUROCRYPT 2018, EUROCRYPT 2018. Lecture Notes in Computer Science, vol. 10821. Springer Cham (2018). https://doi.org/10.1007/978-3-319-78375-8_32017

11. Alper, H.K.: BABE protocol (2020)

12. Stewart, A., Kokoris-Kogia, E.: GRANDPA: a Byzantine Finality Gadget (2020)

13. Gelashvili, R., et al: Block-STM: scaling blockchain execution by turning ordering curse to a performance blessing. In: Proceedings of the 28th ACM SIGPLAN Annual Symposium on Principles and Practice of Parallel Programming (PPoPP 2023), pp. 232–244. Association for Computing Machinery, New York (2023). https://doi.org/10.1145/3572848.3577524

14. Conti, M., Gangwal, A., Todero, M.: Blockchain trilemma solver algorand has dilemma over undecidable messages. In: Proceedings of the 14th International Conference on Availability, Reliability and Security (ARES 2019), Article 16, pp. 1–8. Association for Computing Machinery, New York (2019). https://doi.org/10.1145/3339252.3339255

15. Leonardos, S., Reijsbergen, D., Piliouras, G.: PREStO: a systematic framework for blockchain consensus protocols. IEEE Trans. Eng. Manag. **67**(4), 1028–1044 (2020). https://doi.org/10.1109/TEM.2020.2981286

16. Bonneau, J.: Why blockchain performance is hard to measure (2022)

17. Tasca, P., Tessone, C.J.: A taxonomy of blockchain technologies: principles of identification and classification, Ledger 4 (2019). https://doi.org/10.5195/ledger.2019.140

18. Labazova, O., Dehling, T., Sunyaev, A.: From hype to reality: a taxonomy of blockchain applications. In: Proceedings of the 52nd Hawaii International Conference on System Sciences. IEEE, Wailea (2019)

19. Goundar, S., Chand, S., Chandra, J., Bhardwaj, A., Saber, F.: A taxonomy of blockchain applications. In: Blockchain Technologies, Applications and Cryptocurrencies, pp. 49–71. World Scientific (2020). https://doi.org/10.1142/9789811205279_0003

20. Xu, X., et al.: A taxonomy of blockchain-based systems for architecture design. In: 2017 IEEE International Conference on Software Architecture (ICSA), Gothenburg, Sweden, pp. 243–252 (2017). https://doi.org/10.1109/ICSA.2017.33

21. Bano, S., et al.: SoK: consensus in the age of blockchains. In: Proceedings of the 1st ACM Conference on Advances in Financial Technologies (AFT 2019), pp. 183–198. Association for Computing Machinery, New York (2019). https://doi.org/10.1145/3318041.3355458

22. Bouraga, S.: A taxonomy of blockchain consensus protocols: a survey and classification framework. Expert Syst. Appl. **168**, 114384 (2021). ISSN 0957-4174. https://doi.org/10.1016/j.eswa.2020.114384

23. Nijsse, J.: A taxonomy of blockchain consensus methods. Cryptography **4**(4), 32 (2020). https://doi.org/10.3390/cryptography4040032

24. Garay, J., Kiayias, A.: SoK: a consensus taxonomy in the blockchain era. In: Jarecki, S. (ed.) CT-RSA 2020. LNCS, vol. 12006, pp. 284–318. Springer, Cham (2020). https://doi.org/10.1007/978-3-030-40186-3_13

25. . Cangir, O.F., Cankur, O., Ozsoy, A.: A taxonomy for Blockchain based distributed storage technologies. Inf. Process. Manag. **58**(5) (2021). https://doi.org/10.1016/j.ipm.2021.102627

26. Sarkintudu, S.M., Ibrahim, H.H., Abdwahab, A.B.T.: Taxonomy development of Blockchain platforms: Information systems perspectives. In: AIP Conference Proceedings 2016, 020130 (2018). https://doi.org/10.1063/1.5055532

27. Wang, G., Shi, Z.J., Nixon, M., Han, S.: SoK: sharding on blockchain. In: Proceedings of the 1st ACM Conference on Advances in Financial Technologies (AFT 2019), pp. 41–61. Association for Computing Machinery, New York (2019). https://doi.org/10.1145/3318041.3355457

28. Camenisch, J., Drijvers, M., Hanke, T., Pignolet, Y.A., Shoup, V., Williams, D.: Internet computer consensus. In: Proceedings of the 2022 ACM Symposium on Principles of Distributed Computing (PODC 2022), pp. 81–91. Association for Computing Machinery, New York (2022). https://doi.org/10.1145/3519270.3538430

29. Rocket, T., Yin, M., Sekniqi, K., van Renesse, R., Sirer, E.G.: Scalable and Probabilistic Leaderless BFT Consensus through Metastability (2020). https://doi.org/10.48550/arXiv.1906.08936

30. Kwon, J.: Tendermint: consensus without Mining (2014)

Application and Industry Track

Cadastral: Blockchain-Based Land Registration System

Sagar Suresh[1]([✉]), Kevin Van[1], Chandan Yadav[1], Merlin Jacob[2], and Varsha Wangikar[2]

[1] Department of Computer Engineering, A. P. Shah Institute of Technology Mumbai, Thane, India
{21202012,21202009,20102082}@apsit.edu.in
[2] A. P. Shah Institute of Technology Mumbai, Thane, India
{mjacob,vmwangikar}@apsit.edu.in

Abstract. In an era of evolving property management and ownership practices, blockchain technology emerges as a transformative force and revolutionizes traditional land registration systems. This conceptual approach is a vision of a future world where property transactions occur without glitches. Based on a network of nodes that perform the data distribution, blockchain does not require a central authority (decentralized) and significantly decreases the possibility of data manipulation. Utilizing blockchain's chain of custody and cryptographic features, a land registration system is strongly anticipated to counter existing challenges in the real estate industry, such as fraud, conflicts, and procedural bottlenecks that have been frustrating the industry for decades. The project deploys Solidity-based self-executing smart contracts to automate and enforce agreements related to property transfer, boosting efficiency and cutting out intermediaries. Users self-register and upload the required documents to the system. The critical aspect is that the user is verified only after the inspector meticulously assesses their details using the government database. After assessment, the user can use the application to sell or buy land. The inspector also surveys the land physically before granting permission to make the land available for purchase. The buyer and seller agree on a price before generating the ownership deed. Smart contracts are created for each of these steps from user registration to transfer of ownership, and stored in the local blockchain. Cryptographic algorithm, Hash Algorithm SHA-256 is utilized to protect user's sensitive information and keep anyone from unauthorized access and InterPlanetary File System (IPFS) for file storage.

Keywords: Blockchain · Decentralized · Cryptographic · SHA-256 · IPFS

1 Introduction

Cadastral is a technical term for a comprehensive register of the real estate or real properties of a country, detailing the boundaries and ownership of land. The main problems facing old-fashioned land registration systems are opacity, inefficiency, and susceptibility to, even the invitation of, fraudulent activities. In the old accustomed system, if a user lost original physical agreements which act as concrete proof of the ownership, or if documents get altered or damaged then it isn't very easy to navigate all the details regarding the assets [1]. The outdated land records make it hard to verify land ownership, leading to scams. As a result, several parties assert differing degrees of control over a particular parcel of property [12]. Data accuracy and security are becoming major concerns for all parties involved in land ownership records. These obstacles impede the success rate of land administration, plunging economies into the mire and dampening people's morale regarding real estate deals (Fig. 1).

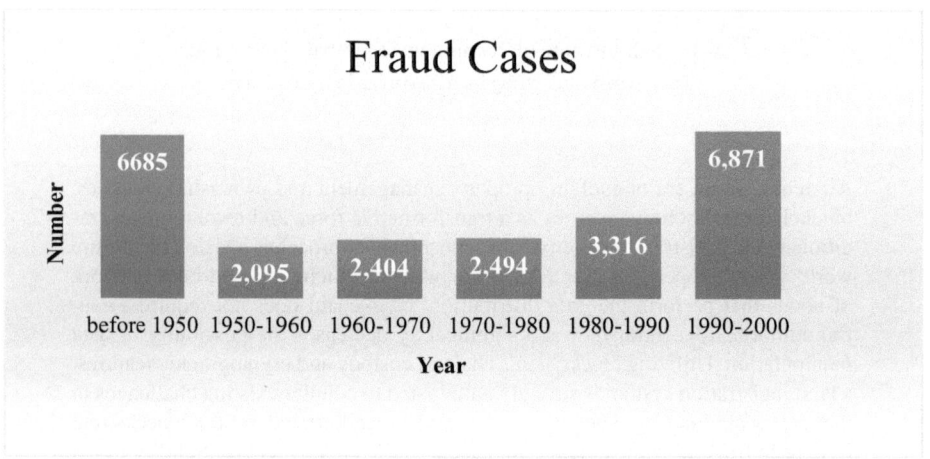

Fig. 1. Statistics of Land fraud cases from the 1950s to 2000s (Source: CaseMine [16])

The above graph depicts the number of various types of land fraud cases in India over decades from the 1950s to the 2000s. While the cases till the 2000s ranged around 7000, the numbers exploded to 170,000 in the following decade. In the next decade, it decreased to around 71,000. The drastic surge in the number of land fraud cases can be due to the rise in industrialization in the country. There is a need to move away from centralized systems and adopt a blockchain-based system to reduce the number of fraud cases [16].

1.1 Blockchain Technology

Blockchain is a revolutionary technology - a distributed ledger technology (DLT) that distributes information across a computer network rather than copies it [3]. It brings out transparency, immutability, and security through security principles like cryptography and consensus mechanisms like Proof of Work (PoW) or Proof of Stake (PoS). The notable functionality comprises smart contracts; which are used to execute the contract electronically, and tokenization, which helps create and transfer digital assets. Each block has a unique identifier and holds the previous block's information. The blockchain operates through peer-to-peer nodes, forming a decentralized and resilient system [11]. Blockchain has been implemented in our project to store innumerable data about property deals, users, and other important information.

1.2   Ethereum

Ethereum is a decentralized blockchain with smart agreement functionality [14]. Although different from Bitcoin, it allows developers to create decentralized apps more effectively and organically as it is robust and decentralized. The currency of Ethereum is called Ether, which is essentially used to pay all the network's fees and computational tasks. Ethereum pulled the idea of smart contracts into the world, a self-executable type of contract regardless of which terms have been put in the codes there is opening up a horde of applications such as decentralized finance (DeFi), non-fungible tokens (NFTs) and decentralized autonomous organizations (DAOs). Ethereum's transition from Proof-of-Work (PoW) to Proof-of-Stake (PoS) offers scalability, low energy consumption, and high-security benefits. Ethereum is best suited for creating a tally that stores deals during the land power transfer process [15].

1.3   Smart Contract

One of the most captivating innovations derived from blockchain is the notion of smart contracts. Such contracts work in the absence of any other party that would develop, write, and execute the contract. When certain conditions are specified, the contract compulsively self-executes, which removes the dependency on a third party as the enforcer of the agreement [15]. Smart contracts integrated into a land registration system streamline land transactions and make property transactions more transparent and secure [13].

Smart contracts have been developed with the idea of providing trust by using digital logic/code. On successful creation or deployment, the smart contract instance is identified by an alphanumeric hash code. This unique hash code can be referred to as a contract address. All of these contract instances have separate private storage [8]. The code of a smart contract consigns a set of rules/logic to take care of the condition of the asset that lies within it. Another advantage of smart contracts is that they operate within the confines of the blockchain network, which means that they automatically get the most out of the blockchain technology, like being immutable and distributed. Each smart contract (as an entity) has its unique address and one can use the address to send or receive the ether (the currency of Ethereum). All smart contract accounts have four properties relevant to them [9]. These four key attributes are given in Table 1.

Table 1. Properties of Smart Contract

Component	Description
Participants	Entities that interact with the contract
Balance	Ether owned by any account
Terms	The conditions of the contract
Code	Machine code for the contract

2 Related Works

[1] The first paper cites that in the common Indian land registration system the brokers are those who function as the accidental third parties between the buyers and the sellers extracting and ready the physical forms for the property transactions. The documents are registered with state ministries, but due to delays, corruption, and inadequate security, there is a risk of document loss or tampering. To overcome these problems, a great emphasis should be laid on blockchain using smart contracts, which simplify the procedures for the transactions and integrate security.

[2] The second paper interprets the Indian land registry system are especially quite known for the controversy centered around the bottlenecks. The multifariousness of the money laundering activities, the many times the applicant demonstrates identifiable patterns, and also the use of multiple middlemen in the laundering process. The application of Blockchain Technology for land registry management overcomes the indicated challenges.

[4] This manuscript focuses on the nature of the land, which is a very important asset, but at the same time may become the cause of many problems. On the one hand, it causes extended ownership disputes and on the other hand, they bust the resources. To tackle these problems part of the system is changed into the Blockchain frame which digitizes and tokenizes assets resolves the matters and helps in the efficient transaction processing using Ethereum.

[5] This paper's essay is to brief us on land ownership registration which is a very tedious and lengthy process in the cases of newly built countries like Bangladesh. This paper highlights some of the drawbacks of traditionally plain registries which include transparency, centralization, authenticity, and also reliability.

[11] This paper states that blockchain technology can streamline land registration by providing a secure, and tamper-proof system that reduces the risk of fraud and corruption. This solution enhances the accessibility and trustworthiness of land ownership records, ensuring efficient and reliable land transfers, particularly in developing countries where traditional processes are prone to inefficiency and disputes.

[12] This paper proposes a land registry system that leverages a decentralized blockchain to securely manage and store property records, utilizing Proof of Stake (PoS) for consensus and SHA-256 for block addressing. It includes dashboards for land inspectors and users to handle registration, verification, and property transfers, ensuring consistency and preventing fraud.

[13] The land registry system is vital for preserving real estate ownership data, but traditional methods are prone to fraud and inefficiency. By integrating QR codes with blockchain technology, this approach aims to enhance the efficiency, transparency, and security of land registration processes.

[15] This manuscript suggests that the current land registry system is prone to fraud and inefficiencies in ownership transfers. A blockchain-based solution is proposed to enhance security, transparency, and efficiency in land registration. By leveraging blockchain's unique features, the system aims to create a decentralized application that addresses these issues while fostering consumer trust.

3 Methodology

Our Cadastral System uses smart contracts and Ethereum to secure the acquisition of user details and land data and facilitate their different operations. Our developed application with Flutter will be user-friendly and will allow the management of land-related information easily. The advent of smart contracts guarantees immutability, transparency, and an accurate trace of all the transactions occurring within the blockchain. Ethereum's decentralized network boosts reliability and survivability in the event of outages or potential cyber-attacks. The inclusion of a pivotal role of the inspector will provide an additional layer of security. Therefore, such an innovative strategy revolves around the process of land registration, transfers of ownership, and any other related entity. The essence of our approach is that our system is developed to ensure that it will provide reliable and adequate management of all the processes of land ownership as well as facilitate land transactions in a digital space. Figure 2 explains the entire flow of the system concerning all the participants involved in the system.

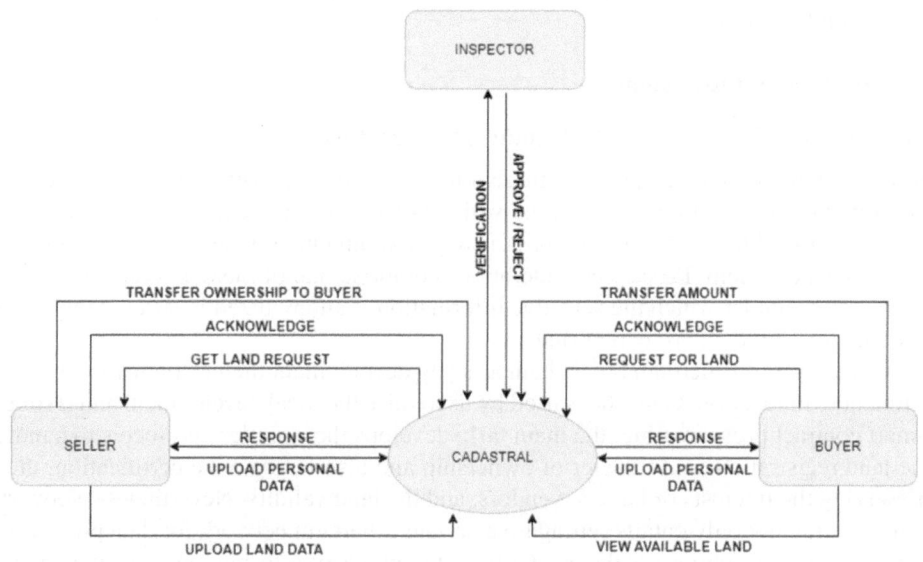

Fig. 2. Cadastral Workflow

3.1 Assumptions

Before getting into the details of our virtual land transfer processing system, it is important to postulate, some of the assumptions about the interaction of this system with the physical world [4]. Those assumptions will govern our system implementation. It is vital to consider criteria like the dependability of data sources, the law existing around the transaction of land, and the trust of the users on digital platforms to perform land-related activities. By correcting such prejudices a priori, we will be enabled to make the system function fully and integrated.

- Coerced modifications: The system lacks a mechanism to verify whether changes by the current owner in land ownership details are made voluntarily or due to external pressure. Because the records are publicly accessible, both the governing authority and citizens can cross-check them at any point.
- Involvement of external finances: The division of land into tokens does not verify the financial transaction through any alternative means. In other words, tokenizing land segments does not provide confirmation or validation of the actual exchange of funds using a different medium.
- Presumption of partnership with government officers: Our system will rely on government officials as well as inspectors to work hand in hand to bring the best out of the system.
- Dependency on government database: The system relies on the national citizenship record system to transfer land ownership to heirs upon the death of a resident. It does not address discrepancies in citizenship record entries.
- Authenticity of existing data: The proposed system operates under the impression that the information about the present ownership of land and property by residents is inherently genuine.

3.2   Modules of the System

3.2.1   Data Collection and Blockchain Infrastructure

To virtually revolutionize the land transaction process, the integrity and security of every step for smooth functioning is ensured which is the crux of our methodology. First of all, Cadastral obtains the land records using government officials and even individual landowners' help. Privacy considerations comprise one of the core elements of the methodology under which the sensitive information is anonymized in strict compliance with the relevant data protection rules.

Our choice of Ethereum blockchain as a key development theme confirms our commitment to innovation. Ganache is used by us to raise the local development and testing. Smart contract programming, the main task, develops the agentless protocols to handle the land registration, and transfer of ownership and also validate the certification, thus preserving the interests of buyers, vendors, and the land validity. Nevertheless, network configuration not only entails setting up a private Ethereum network for data protection but also as well as observing the most efficient methods of information security and privacy. Thus, this holistic strategy indicates the caliber of our mission of redefining land transfers through the combination of outstanding technologies and also consideration for ethical aspects.

3.2.2   Seller and Buyer Dashboard

After the whole process has been completed, the verified sellers can enter our system which enables them to enlist their land for sale. After the land is verified by our inspector, buyers can survey for lands and are provided with a large source of data which includes: the city, price, area, state, and precise photos of the land. After the issuance of the permit, the land can be publicized and sold leading to a rise in the confidence of the sellers who will be able to complete the transaction. Among many things we can mention, a fair and properly organized land ownership transfer would include an inspector who would be officially directing all these processes, hence, protecting the seller against fraudulent activity by the buyer and vice versa.

3.2.3 Inspector

The Inspector, a local police officer or a representative of the government, officiates two critical tasks in our land registration system. Firstly, upon buyer and seller registration, crucial personal details, including name, age, city, email, passport number, and the Aadhaar card, are communicated to the inspector. The Aadhaar details serve as a reliable source for user verification, and based on this data, the inspector determines whether a user is eligible to proceed further. Secondly, land data such as survey number, property ID, quality of the area, and price undergo validation by the inspector. Before validation, the inspector physically surveys the property to examine it, ensuring it aligns with the details provided and complies with legal requirements. Once verified, buyers gain the ability to bid for the property. Upon the buyer's decision to purchase, the inspector oversees the proper transfer of ownership to the buyer and facilitates the financial transaction to the seller. The role and involvement of the inspector in different aspects of the cadastral system are depicted below in Table 2.

Table 2. Roles of Inspector

Roles	Permission
Registration of users	✕
Verification of registered users	✓
Verification of land documents	✓
Involvement in deal	✕
Supervise and final stamp of deal and title transfer	✓

3.2.4 Smart Contract

In this innovative land registration system, incorporating blockchain technology brings forth heightened security and efficiency. Upon buyer and seller registration, sensitive personal and property data is securely stored on the decentralized blockchain. The Aadhaar number, a pivotal identifier, undergoes hashing for a verifiable and unalterable record, ensuring robust user verification through smart contracts. During property validation, key details are recorded on the tamper-resistant blockchain ledger, providing a transparent and fraud-resistant repository of information. Smart contracts further streamline the ownership transfer process, triggering automatic smart contract execution upon buyer payment, eliminating intermediaries, and reducing transaction time and costs. This implementation transforms the land registration process, leveraging blockchain's transparency and automation to establish a secure and trustworthy foundation for property transactions (Fig. 3).

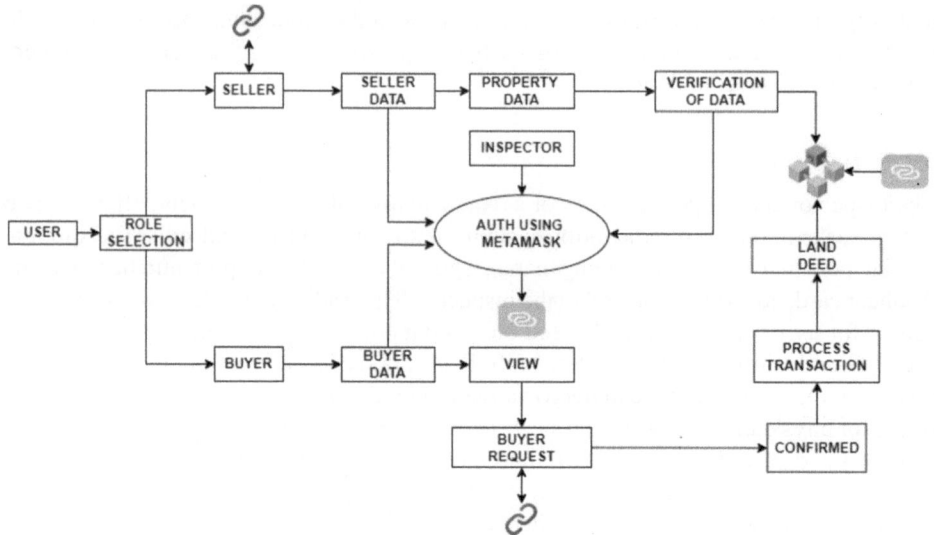

Fig. 3. Smart contract

4 Results

The implementation of our innovative land registration system showcases tangible results in revolutionizing the traditional process. The system ensures secure storage of sensitive data, transparent property validation, and automated ownership transfers. Buyer and seller dashboards, coupled with the crucial role of the inspector, contribute to a streamlined, fraud-resistant, and trustworthy transaction environment. The use of smart contracts reduces intermediary involvement while enhancing efficiency. As we witness successful land transactions and the creation of an unchangeable record on the blockchain, the results underscore the potential of our approach to reshaping the landscape of property management and ownership in the Web3 era.

Figures 4 and 5 display the user dashboard. In Fig. 4, the user has not been verified yet and therefore cannot partake in the application. The tabs add land, land gallery are not accessible to the user. After the user is verified, the user will be displayed a verified mark (shown in Fig. 5) onto which the user can proceed further and indulge in the application.

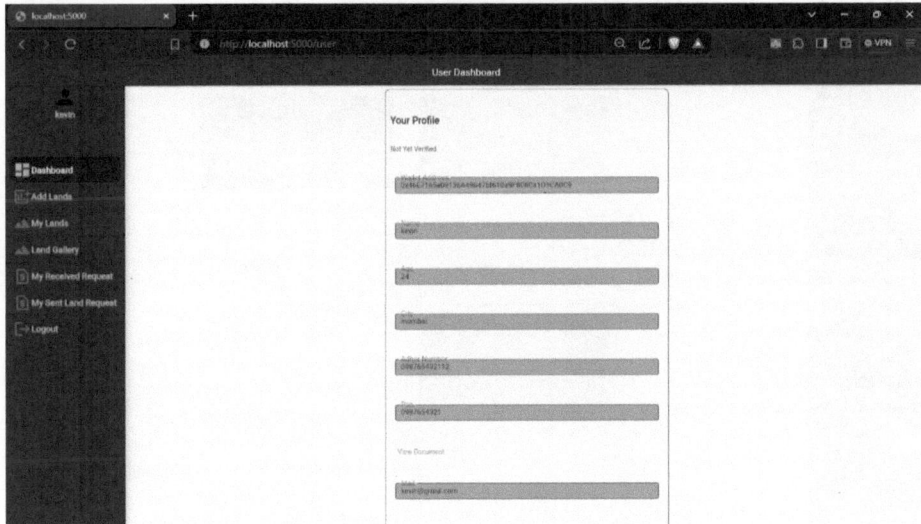

Fig. 4. User Dashboard (Unverified)

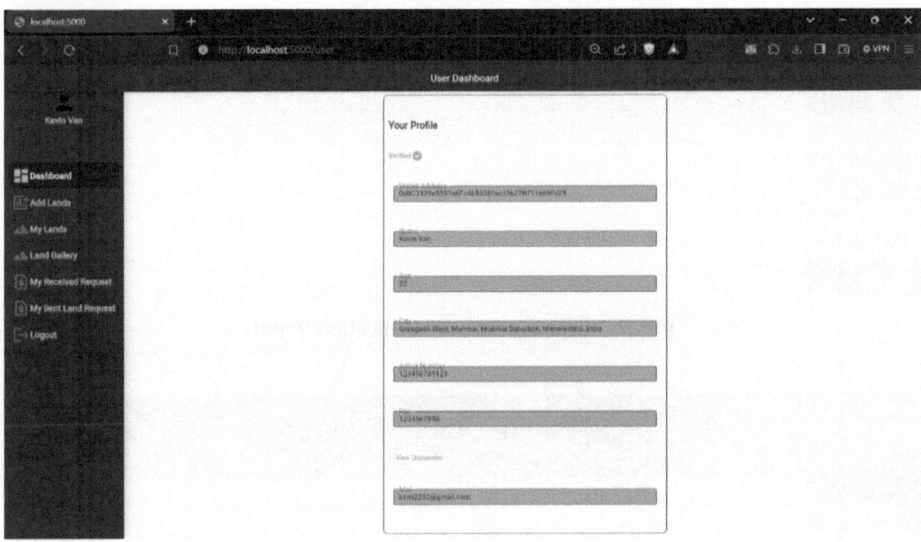

Fig. 5. User Dashboard (verified)

Figure 6 showcases the Land Gallery, where users can browse all available lands for purchase. They can view land details, send purchase requests to sellers, and, upon request approval, submit price bids. Sellers have the option to accept or reject these requests.

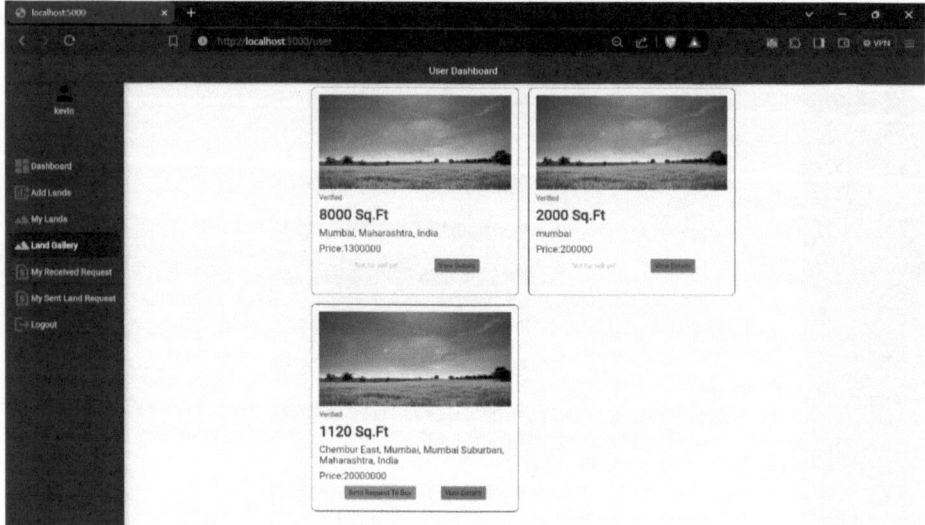

Fig. 6. Users' Land Gallery

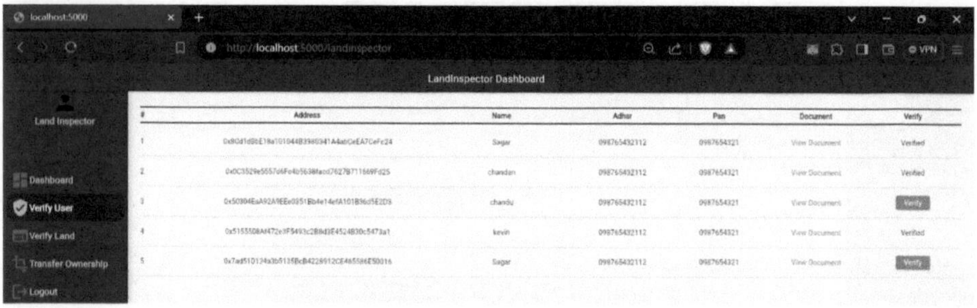

Fig. 7. Inspectors' User Verification Portal

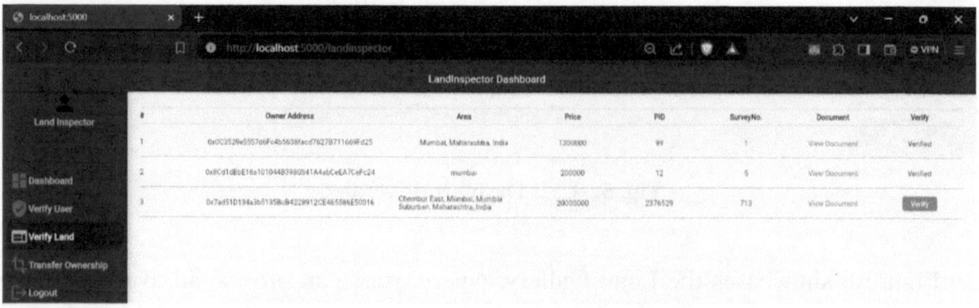

Fig. 8. Inspectors' Land Verification Portal

Figure 7 illustrates the inspectors' dashboard, where they monitor user interactions and access complete user profiles, including documents like Aadhaar card details.

Inspectors can query government authorities and verify user information through official databases. After thorough verification, they authorize users to engage in the platform's activities. In Fig. 8, inspectors use the dashboard to conduct land inspections too. They perform physical surveys, verify documents, and provide a permissibility opinion on the area. After a thorough evaluation, they authorize the land for sale, ensuring regulatory compliance and preventing dubious transactions.

The proposed application is an innovative solution that solves the intricacies of various parameters in existing systems. Land evaluation is carried out through objective rather than subjective approaches which realign views to an evaluation system with physical surveys, document checking, and standardized data collection methods. Improved communication is achieved through the recycling of information, and real-time updates on transactions in progress. At the same time, it is ensured that the transactions meet legal requirements at every stage. Stringent security procedures will keep all types of information in a safe condition. The result may serve as a new benchmark of reliability and credibility in real estate securities management.

The following table showcases the differences in various parameters concerning the existing and our proposed system (Table 3).

Table 3. Differences between the existing and proposed system

Parameter	Existing	Proposed
Decentralization	No	Yes
Security	Low	High
Additional security	No	Yes
Mediator involvement and cost	High	Low
Scalability	Low	High

- Decentralization
  We adopted blockchain technology to the existing land registry system, thus preventing the external parties from manipulating the records. Moreover, blockchain technology performs its operations on a shared ledger system that enables all the network participants to view the common set of records. This level of decentralization in contrast to the relatively low decentralization presented in the current land registry system can reduce the chances of tampering.
- Security
  Every land record is stored and maintained inside the smart contracts (nodes) of the blockchain. Since the records cannot be accessed by anyone, they are secured. Only the inspector can see the land details upon verification of said land. The buyers need to request permission from the seller to get the entire details regarding the land. Thus, a blockchain-based system provides high security.
- Additional Security
  The inclusion of an inspector has a big impact considering the proposed system. The inspector verifies the user and land details to validate the genuineness of the user and

the authenticity of the land respectfully. Therefore, the inspector acts as a two-step verification that provides additional security and fends off any illegitimate users.

- Mediator involvement and cost

  Mediators or brokers are the people who carry out the entire process and guide the buyer and seller in the land transfer business. The existing land registration system heavily depends on such mediators. As part of the deal, mediators get their commission via the person they are representing. The proposed system equipped with blockchain technology cuts down the number of mediators involved in transferring assets from one user to another. As a result, it eliminates any costs or commissions viable to the broker.

- Scalability

  The system is constructed to efficiently manage an increased volume of land registrations with ease. The functions within the smart contracts are optimized to address scalability concerns effectively. Consequently, the proposed model exhibits a high level of scalability.

5 Conclusion

In conclusion, our research explores the transformative potential of implementing a blockchain-based land registration system, addressing critical issues prevalent in traditional methods. By leveraging blockchain's decentralized nature, cryptographic security, and smart contracts, our system offers a paradigm shift in property transactions. The tamper-resistant blockchain ledger ensures transparency, while smart contracts streamline processes, reducing fraud and intermediaries. The buyer and seller dashboards, integrated with a crucial inspector's role, create a collaborative and secure environment. As we imagine a future where land transactions are seamlessly recorded in immutable blockchain blocks, our project signifies a significant step towards revolutionizing and establishing trust in the property management domain.

References

1. Gollapalli, S.A., Krishnamoorthy, G., Jagtap, N.S., Shaikh, R.: Land registration system using block-chain. In: International Conference on Smart Innovations in Design, Environment, Management, Planning and Computing (ICSIDEMPC) 2020, pp. 242–247. IEEE, Aurangabad (2020). https://doi.org/10.1109/ICSIDEMPC49020.2020.9299606
2. Suganthe, R.C., Shanthi, N., Latha, R.S., Gowtham, K., Deepakkumar, S., Elango, R.: Blockchain enabled digitization of land registration. In: International Conference on Computer Communication and Informatics (ICCCI) 2021, pp. 1–5. IEEE, Coimbatore (2021). https://doi.org/10.1109/ICCCI50826.2021.9402469
3. Shinde, D., Padekar, S., Raut, S., Wasay, A., Sambhare, S.S.: Land registry using blockchain - a survey of existing systems and proposing a feasible solution. In: 5th International Conference On Computing, Communication, Control And Automation (ICCUBEA) 2019, pp. 1–6. IEEE, Pune (2019). https://doi.org/10.1109/ICCUBEA47591.2019.9129289
4. Nandi, M., Bhattacharjee, R.K., Jha, A., Barbhuiya, F.A.: A secured land registration framework on Blockchain. In: Third ISEA Conference on Security and Privacy (ISEA-ISAP) 2020, pp. 130–138. IEEE, Guwahati (2020). https://doi.org/10.1109/ISEA-ISAP49340.2020.235011

5. Islam, M.S., Iqbal, F.S., Islam, M.: A novel framework for implementation of land registration and ownership management via blockchain in Bangladesh. In: IEEE Region 10 Symposium (TENSYMP) 2020, pp. 859–862. IEEE, Dhaka (2020). https://doi.org/10.1109/TENSYMP50 017.2020.9230721

6. Majumdar, M.A., Monim, M., Shahriyer, M.M.: Blockchain based land registry with delegated proof of stake (DPoS) consensus in Bangladesh. In: IEEE Region 10 Symposium (TENSYMP) 2020, pp. 1756–1759. IEEE, Dhaka (2020). https://doi.org/10.1109/TENSYMP50017.2020. 9230612

7. Mendi, A.F., Sakaklı, K.K., Çabuk, A.: A blockchain based land registration system proposal for Turkey. In: 4th International Symposium on Multidisciplinary Studies and Innovative Technologies (ISMSIT) 2020, pp. 1–6. IEEE, Istanbul (2020). https://doi.org/10.1109/ISM SIT50672.2020.9255078

8. Kadam, R., Vidhani, V., Bane, A., Valecha, B., Giri, N.: Land records system using hybrid blockchain. In: International Conference on Convergence to Digital World - Quo Vadis (ICCDW) 2020, pp. 1–4. IEEE, Mumbai (2020). https://doi.org/10.1109/ICCDW45521.2020. 9318693

9. Biswas, M., Faysal, J.A., Ahmed, K.A.: LandChain: a blockchain based secured land registration system. In: International Conference on Science & Contemporary Technologies (ICSCT) 2021, pp. 1–6. IEEE, Dhaka (2021). https://doi.org/10.1109/ICSCT53883.2021.9642505

10. Umrao, L.S.: Blockchain-based reliable framework for land registration information system. IJTD 13(1), 1–16 (2022). https://doi.org/10.4018/IJTD.300743

11. Mansoor, M.A., Ali, M., Mateen, A., Kaleem, M., Nazir, S.: Blockchain technology for land registry management in developing countries. In: 2023 2nd International Conference on Emerging Trends in Electrical, Control, and Telecommunication Engineering (ETECTE), Lahore, Pakistan, pp. 1–6 (2023). https://doi.org/10.1109/ETECTE59617.2023.10396736

12. Maragiri, S.B., Harsha, P., Mamatha, K.R.: Blockchain based land registration system with hierarchy maintenance. Int. J. Eng. Res. Technol. (IJERT) 12(06) (2023)

13. Singh, P., Verma, P., Chuphal, T., Chakraverti, A., Singh, M.K.: Secure and reliable land registry system using QR code and blockchain technology. Int. J. Eng. Res. Technol. (IJERT) 13(4) (2024)

14. Lavanya Shree, D.P., Harish, T.A., Shantala, C.P.: Secure land registry system using ethereum blockchain. IJFMR 6(4) (2024)

15. Blockchain based land registry system. Int. J. Novel Res. Dev. 8(4), f252–f257 (2023). ISSN: 2456-4184, www.ijnrd.org

16. www.casemine.com/search/in/title%3Aland%2Bfraud%2Bcase

Author Index

A
Anh, N. T. 95

B
Bang, N. H. 95
Borse, Snehal 50
Bui, Dinh-Ngoc 109

C
Choy, Shi Hong 3
Chu, Dongliang 33

D
Do, Thuat 69, 109

F
Fan, Xinxin 3

G
Guo, Bing 84

H
He, Sheng 16
He, Songlin 33, 84
Ho, Nicholas 3
Huang, Qinglin 16
Hung, N. N. 95

J
Jacob, Merlin 123
Jia, Daiwei 84
Jiao, Shaoshuai 16

K
Khanh, H. V. 95
Khoa, T. D. 95

L
Lin, Jinxuan 16
Lin, Zepeng 16
Loc, V. C. P. 95
Lyu, Xukang 33

N
Ngan, T. K. N. 95

P
Pham, Tuan-Anh 69

R
Ren, Jun 16

S
Shyamasundar, R. K. 50
Sun, Yufang 84
Suresh, Sagar 123

T
Tan, Teik Guan 3
Tran, Tuan 69
Triet, M. N. 95

U
Ummair, Mohammad 50

V
Van, Kevin 123

J. Feng et al. (Eds.): ICBC 2024, LNCS 15425, pp. 137–138, 2025.
https://doi.org/10.1007/978-3-031-77095-1

W
Wangikar, Varsha   123

X
Xiong, Dengbin   16

Y
Yadav, Chandan   123

Z
Zhang, Liang-Jie   16